Tomorrow's Television
An examination of British broadcasting
past, present and future

D1784206

Where is television going? Where is it taking us?
People care deeply about what they – and their
children – are going to watch. Who controls what
is on the TV screen in our living-room today . . .
and tomorrow? These are the vital questions
examined by the government-appointed Annan
Committee, whose findings will have far-reaching
effects.

TV Producer Andrew Quicke writes with an
insider's knowledge of the key people and events.
He takes a lively, informed look at TV in Britain:
the hidden factors behind news selection; the
accusations of bias and vested interest; levels of
screen sex and violence; censorship and politics.

After drawing up a comprehensive picture of the
origins and development of British television from
Reith to Lord Hill, the author concludes with an
Open Letter to Lord Annan, setting out detailed
and constructive recommendations for the future.

Andrew Quicke's TV experience has been in
Schools' television, as director of *Panorama* with
Richard Dimbleby, and as acting editor of *The
Money Programme*. He has had a spell in an East
End soap factory, at the Central Office of
Information and as a Christian youth club leader.
He is currently executive producer with a
newsfilm agency.

To my mother and father

An Aslan Book

Tomorrow's Television

An examination of British broadcasting
past, present and future

Andrew Quicke

 **Lion Publishing**

Copyright © Andrew Quicke 1976

LION PUBLISHING
121 High Street, Berkhamsted, Herts

First edition 1976

ISBN 0 85648 060 6

Cover illustration: BBC copyright photograph
Illustrations 1, 3 and 4 by permission of *Punch*;
illustrations 2 and 6 by permission of London
Express News and Feature Services; illustration
5 by permission of Mark Boxer.

Printed in Great Britain by
Hazell Watson & Viney Ltd, Aylesbury, Bucks

Contents

Illustrations

Preface

This book makes no claims in the area of original research into the problems of television. Instead it is intended to give the general reader an insight into the complexities and the politics of the television world, and to explain some of the problems affecting the future of television in Britain that will have to be solved by the Committee looking into the future of television under the chairmanship of Lord Annan.

I must record my indebtedness to other authors who have written so informatively about the history of television and its achievements. In particular I would thank Peter Black and Milton Shulman, perhaps the two best television critics, and Anthony Smith, the former editor of *24 Hours*, whose writings have been among the best on the subject.

Personal thanks are due to Carole Martin, who struggled with the typing of the manuscript. I should add a final word of thanks to all those colleagues who have made fourteen years in the television and documentary film industry such a pleasant and rewarding experience.

Chapter One

Television under Attack

' "You might just as well say," added the March Hare, "that I like what I get is the same thing as I get what I like." ' *Alice Through the Looking-Glass*

On the whole, nowadays the British public do get what they like on their television sets. BBC 1 and ITV carry up to fifteen hours of broadcasting every day, BBC 2 slightly less. According to BBC audience research the working class spend on average 20 hours per week watching television.[1] At the time of that survey 41 per cent of the working class watched BBC, and 59 per cent watched ITV. The lower middle class on average watched slightly less, and slightly preferred the BBC. They watched sixteen evening hours per week, divided into 57 per cent to BBC and 43 per cent to ITV. You might have expected the number of hours spent watching television by the upper middle class to have been considerably fewer. But it seems that our upper middle class spends no less than fourteen hours a week watching television, preferring to watch BBC rather than ITV in the ratio of 66 per cent to 34 per cent. It all adds up to a lot of time spent watching television.

Viewers' choice

For sporting programmes audiences often rise to 21 million, and for the World Cup Final to a staggering 31 million. Drama and light entertainment programmes can draw up to 16 million, while news and current affairs can draw audiences of up to 12 million. The television audience does not greatly care for opera, ballet, religious and educational programmes. Audiences for these seldom exceed two or three million.

BBC 2 began by attempting to provide minority-taste programmes which were not given a slot on BBC 1. For example, Tuesday evening was given over entirely to adult education, and other evenings developed specific themes. This was not a success. Now the policy is to provide alternative programmes to BBC 1. Usually BBC 2 audiences are half the size of those of either of the other two channels. (There are exceptions to this. On Monday nights BBC 2 can pull in an audience of five million for a western when the other two channels are pitting their heavyweight current affairs programmes *Panorama* and *World in Action* against each other.) Robin Scott, former Controller, BBC 2, admitted that for BBC 2 he considered 15 per cent of the total audience to be satisfactory. BBC 2 minority-interest programmes include such subjects as cricket, golf, motoring, archaeology, finance, sociology, foreign feature films and rugby league – although by no means all of these subjects could be regarded as the preserve of an intellectual *élite*.

Recently the Independent Broadcasting Authority (IBA), together with the existing programme contractors, have demanded a second channel for ITV on the grounds that they, too, want the freedom to provide 'choice' through alternative programming. It so happens that until 1971 little was heard of this demand to cater for the minority viewer. But as advertising revenues rose during the same period that the government levy on advertising revenue to ITV companies was reduced, they felt they would be able to sell the extra advertising time that a second ITV channel would provide.

Sir John Eden announced at the Advertising Film Ball at the Dorchester Hotel in March 1973 that, as Conservative Minister for Posts and Telecommunications, he confidently expected to be able to announce his plans for the fourth channel in 1974. Meanwhile he welcomed suggestions from the industry as to how it should be used. A roar of approval went up from the assembled guests of the advertising industry at this clear hint that the Conservative Party would continue to support the forces of free enterprise, by providing them with as many channels as their all-too-successful rivals, the government-sponsored, but inconveniently independent-minded, BBC. When Labour won the election at the end of the month, it became clear that no decision about the allocation of the fourth channel would be made until the re-constituted Committee of Enquiry, under Lord Annan, had reported.

The structure of broadcasting

In November 1972 the BBC celebrated its fiftieth birthday by unleashing on a tolerant public an orgy of uncritical nostalgia more suitable for the death of a sovereign. Its income from licences totals £185 million a year for its broadcasting services (radio no longer exacts a separate licence fee). West German and French TV are now better financed than the BBC. Both the BBC and the ITV companies are permitted to function as broadcasters by virtue of a licence issued by the Minister of Posts and Telecommunications (formerly by the Postmaster-General) under the terms of the Wireless Telegraphy Act, 1949, and the Telegraph Act, 1869. By granting these licences the government gives monopoly rights in the field of public-service broadcasting to the BBC, and monopoly rights in the field of broadcasting not paid for out of licence revenue to the IBA.

The BBC's Charter, last granted in 1964 and now extended until 1981, defines the purpose of the BBC. The reasons why 'Elizabeth the Second by Grace of God, of Great Britain, Ireland, the British Dominions beyond the seas, Queen' was moved to 'will, ordain and declare' the renewal of the Charter were twofold. First:

'It has been made to appear to Us that some fifteen and three-quarter million licences have been issued in Our United Kingdom of Great Britain and Northern Ireland, the Channel Islands and the Isle of Man to install and use apparatus for wireless telegraphy for the purpose of receiving broadcast programmes.'

And second:

'The widespread interest which is thereby and other evidences shown to be taken by Our peoples in the broadcasting services,' and 'the great value of such services as means of disseminating information, education and entertainment.'

Noting the popular demand (it is rumoured that the royal family watch a lot of television – though the Queen has nothing to do with the wording of the Act) the Sovereign directed that the BBC should 'continue to provide broadcasting services subject to such licences and agreements . . . as Our Postmaster-General may from time to time grant or make with the Corporation'.

The BBC, in strict terms of law, consists of the twelve governors, appointed technically by the Queen in Council, but effectively by the Cabinet Office. The governors appoint the Director-General of the BBC as their chief executive officer. Until the appointment of Lord Hill as Chairman of the Board of Governors the Director-General was effectively king. Lord Hill soon made it clear that, as Chairman, he was keen to take an active role in shaping policy, and some believe that his arrival precipitated the then Director-General Sir Hugh Greene's resignation in 1970.

The BBC's revenue comes not as a grant from the exchequer but from the revenue collected by the Post Office, which issues broadcast-receiving licences. At present the Post Office collects around £186 million and passes on to the BBC around £176 million. The Minister of Posts and Telecommunications has never banned a particular BBC programme, though frequently asked by MPs to intervene. The situation could be described as one of trust, with the veto of the Minister as ultimate deterrent.

Perhaps the crucial distinction between the BBC and the Independent Broadcasting Authority lies in the nature of their founding documents; the former being permissive, the latter restrictive. The Independent Broadcasting Authority has sole power to grant licences to commercial companies in the various regions to provide 'television broadcasting services as a public service for disseminating information, education and entertainment'. If that seems identical to the BBC Charter, there is an important extra clause which is not imposed on the BBC. IBA programmes shall 'maintain a high standard in all respects . . . and a proper balance and wide range in their subject matter'. They shall include nothing which 'offends against good taste or decency, or is likely to encourage or incite to crime, or lead to disorder, or be offensive to public feeling.' It is up to the IBA to determine what offends against good taste.

In a celebrated incident in 1973 a private citizen successfully succeeded in postponing the broadcast of a controversial film about Andy Warhol, by appealing to the High Court. Their Lordships in due course decided that it was the sole duty of the IBA to decide what was offensive to public feeling, and that private individuals could not intervene in such a decision by appealing to the High Court. The programme was subsequently shown and claimed a record audience for a late-night programme of 18 million, most of them more disappointed than shocked.

The second vital difference between the BBC and the ITV companies is in their methods of finance. The Independent Broadcasting Authority draws its income from rent paid to it by the programme companies or 'contractors', as they are called because they 'contract' to provide television broadcasting for the various regions for a given number of years. The contractors earn their income from the sale of advertising air-time, limited by the IBA to a given number of minutes in any one hour. Sponsorship of programmes by advertisers, practised in the United States, is specifically prohibited in the UK by Act of Parliament. The exchequer gains a handsome income from ITV – the figure for 1972 exceeding £50 million. Not only are the companies' profits taxed, but the 'levy', an additional tax on the companies, has been collected for the exchequer by the IBA. In addition the IBA pays tax on its own income from the companies: to the tune of £3,856,000 in 1974.

Two such powerful bodies as the BBC and IBA would

seem to have little to fear from their critics. Criticism can come from such people as newspaper columnists and small pressure groups – often short of funds and of questionable authority. But Parliament has to decide before 1981 whether or not to maintain broadcasting in its present form and dissenters are bound to be noted by the television establishment. It will be politicians thinking of their votes, and probably acting on the results of an enquiry such as that of the Annan Committee, who will shape the future of British broadcasting until the end of the century.

Many in the Labour Party have no great love for either broadcasting establishment, disliking what they regard as the arrogance of the BBC as much as the commercialism of the IBA, whose creation they once opposed. The Conservatives have often believed the BBC to be run by a band of loose-living 'lefties', and created both commercial television and now commercial radio to compete with, and lessen the influence of, the BBC. Both parties are anxious not to affront the 'moral conscience of the nation'. The reappointment of the Annan Committee in 1974 was in answer to repeated calls by protesters for an investigation into the whole structure of broadcasting as we know it in Britain today. (The Annan Committee was first appointed in 1970, but dissolved by the Heath government.)

Who are these protesters and what are they protesting about?

Moral Protest: The National Viewers' and Listeners' Association (NVALA)

Brian Groombridge, an IBA executive, once described the NVALA as a 'section of conscientious and vigilant viewers'. (Not everyone has been so charitable about them.) Led by an energetic housewife and ex-schoolteacher, Mrs Mary Whitehouse, with support from other guardians of the national conscience – among them Malcolm Muggeridge and Lord Longford – the NVALA has frequently protested about the violence and sexual activities seen on television. They believe that many programmes deliberately subvert

Christian values. They deplore much modern television drama, especially on BBC, and in particular regard the BBC *Wednesday Plays* as encouraging sexual permissiveness, and anti-family and anti-authority attitudes. They are deeply worried about sex education television programmes in schools. They see much television as providing a platform for free-thinkers to advocate powerfully a permissive morality.

They would agree with writers like James McMillan: 'Probably the vast majority of people in the West would deplore further weakening of conventional – or what was once conventional – morality. But they follow in the wake of the present persuasive, eminently reasonable advocates of the new order.'[2]

Malcolm Muggeridge, a relatively recent convert to Christianity, has been more specific about the action to be taken: 'When the persuasion to turn away from what we believe to be the true morality is intrusive, it should be restricted.'

Some of the most eloquent cataloguing of television's defects has come from an Anglican priest of literary skill and discernment, Gavin Reid. Reid is closer to the forces of radical protest than to the forces of puritanism, and he would not claim to speak for the 'silent majority'. He writes: 'When one adds up the sheer output of programmes that portray socially abnormal heterosexual relations then it would appear that a case can be made for the undermining influence of television on western society's values . . . By concentrating on the contents of television programmes rather than the nature of the medium itself, government and voluntary bodies have totally misunderstood the nature of television's threat to civilization. What is needed is for legislation to cut back transmission hours and for massive public education programmes similar to those now being conducted to dissuade people from smoking.'[3]

In part Reid seems to be referring to the alleged danger that television affects the individual's imagination so persuasively that it constitutes an assault on our individuality and integrity. He asks further: 'Is too much television a distraction from the development of an authentic inner being? Is too much television journalism a distraction from the development of social being and action?'

What appears clear is that there is an articulate protest movement based on Christian values, which sincerely believes that television must be controlled by an outside body to prevent what it regards as excesses committed by both television authorities (but particularly the BBC). The movement scored perhaps its first success in the decision by the BBC governors to set up an independent Complaints Commission in 1971. This step took the steam out of a demand, known to have backing within the Conservative Party, for the setting up of some such authoritative body as a Broadcasting Council. Such a Council could have eroded the freedom of broadcasters, or what the *Daily Mail* television critic, Peter Black, called 'the responsibility of the broadcasters', and thereby permanently damaged the BBC. Black claims that the BBC appeared 'to surrender a fragment, without giving away a thing'. BBC producers inside television, and NVALA members outside broadcasting would probably both agree.

But the NVALA viewers want more. From their perspective of the Christian ethic they want specific programmes to 'promote their somewhat theocratic version of Christianity'.[4] Politicians who would like to gain greater control over television by the government are prepared to support their demands.

The politicians

'Television is too important to be left to the broadcasters.' So said Tony Benn, in a phrase that has since become famous. Many politicians from both Right and Left feel aggrieved by what they take to be the bias and disrespect that infect many programmes dealing with politics and politicians. They resent leading political reporters such as Robin Day, who more and more assert their role as advocates of the people, constantly reaffirming that 'the public have the right to know'. Both sides of industry would agree with Benn, when he claims that: 'almost all we see of trade unionists or business leaders are hurried little street interviews, when they are pinned against a wall by a battery of accusing microphones'. Even within the media there is support for his position. The main film and television union, ACTT, has done an important piece of research into television news bias.'

Criticism of television is by no means restricted to the Labour Party. Peregrine Worsthorne, political columnist of the *Sunday Telegraph*, spoke for many Conservative MPs when he appeared in a *Talkback* programme with Sir Charles Curran, Director-General of the BBC. Worsthorne argued that the BBC's status as a body financed by the public ought to bar it from engaging in programmes that it knows may provoke large numbers of that public. Curran retorted: 'Are you suggesting that no public body can ever tell the truth about this country? If so, I think that is one of the most corrupt doctrines I have ever heard.' BBC and ITV producers have come to accept as a fact of life that both political parties will protest vociferously from time to time about real or imaginary grievances, and that this is healthy.

Outside the usual confines of party politics, the New Left attacks television at a deeper level. Professor Herbert Marcuse, in his important book *One-Dimensional Man*, has argued that the values of our capitalistic, advanced-industrial society are so entwined with the basic assumptions and value judgements of television and the print-media that the public are conditioned into accepting the *status quo* without question. Marcuse believes that it is the unquestioned assumptions behind the programmes, rather than the statements made on the programmes, that are likely to find a home in people's minds. He cites such books as Vance Packard's *The Hidden Persuaders*, *The Status Seekers* and *The Waste-Makers*, and William H. Whyte's *The Organisation Man* as popular analyses of the problem of 'one-dimensional man' processed by the media.

'In the medium of technology, culture, politics and the economy merge into an omni-present system which swallows up or repulses all alternatives. Perhaps the most telling evidence can be obtained by simply looking at television or listening to the radio for one consecutive hour for a couple of days, not shutting off the commercials, and now and then switching the station.' [6]

The critique of television developed by the New Left expands Marcuse's two closely related theses, those of 'manipulation' and of 'repressive tolerance'. The argument goes like this: television is a reductive medium, bringing down to the same level of unreality political discussion, quiz competitions, World Cup matches and Miss World contests. In all of these the competitive element, the hallmark of capitalist and *élitist* societies, is stressed, and all are treated with the same degree of seriousness. Michael Aspel at the Miss World contest is every bit as portentous as Robin Day on election night. If everything is equally important, then nothing is important.

Many New Left radicals, accepting this critique, refuse to appear on television – though those other critics, the churchmen and the politicians, never seem to hesitate. New Left radicals believe that television's power is reinforced by the nature of viewing patterns, in a society which is atomized into tiny family groups. The manipulators' images of life, politics and culture are limited to carefully defined areas, and projected into homes with the approval and consent of the ruling class.

Much of the political indoctrination achieved by television is due to its limitation of politics to very narrowly defined areas. These could be roughly equated with the area of consensus politics embraced by the three largest parties. Fascists, Communists and Anarchists are prevented from appearing on programmes month in, month out. Sir Oswald Mosley was for a long period totally banned from appearing on BBC, even though his ideas on Europe deserved a hearing. Extremist racial groups were, until recently, ostracized by television producers. Today one brand of racialism gets plentiful airing through the frequent appearances of Mr Enoch Powell, who is too intelligent a man ever to risk transgressing the clauses of the Race Relations Act. By selecting Powell as the sole exponent of a racialist viewpoint, television has implied that his views can be discounted as those of a lunatic fringe. In fact, an important minority of the Conservative Party and of the working class share his views – witness the dockers' march to Parliament Square in 1968 in support of Powellite views.

If Powell is the only figure of stature on the far Right who gains access to the television screens to express his views, what figure on the far Left ever breaks into the cosy atmosphere of *Panorama*, *This Week* and *Tonight*? Interestingly enough, these programmes tend to have mildly leftist editors. For example, Philip Whitehead of *This Week* is now Labour MP for Derby North. But no figure of stature from the revolutionary Left ever appears. Those who would advocate the overthrow of parliamentary democracy are simply not invited.

I can recall only two exceptions to this generalization. At the time of the potentially revolutionary riots in France in 1968, Anthony Smith of *24 Hours* imported Daniel Cohn-Bendit to discuss the radical protest movement in France, and its implications for British radicals. The result was a more genuine discussion of radical ideas on television (for a programme with an audience of around five million) than can have appeared on British television since its inception. The second occasion was when David Frost invited Jerry Rubin and his Yippies on to his programme. A riot ensued, and Frost retreated to a second prepared studio.

The radical challenge to the concept of permitting only 'safe' consensus politics goes much further than getting left-wing speakers on the screen. Critics like Professor Stuart Hood and Christians like Gavin Reid would both agree that the constant propaganda of materialist advertising is as harmful as political limitation. Thirty second or one minute 'spots', which suggest that sexual gratification and love can be bought by drinking the right beverages, wearing the right perfumes or using the right bath salts, represent only the surface of television's materialist outlook.

Hood writes, 'More damaging are the implicit assumptions that underlie the telefilms, the teleplays and the comedy shows which subject the viewer to a view of the world where emotion is supreme and where thought is discounted, where the symbols of success are material and sexual, where certain staid forms of virtue will always triumph over the paper tigers of evil, and fundamentally the individual can best live by accepting the established order.'[7]

The implications are disturbing. We know that small children start TV-viewing at the age of four or even earlier. Research has shown that for many children their weekly viewing hours can easily exceed the number of hours they spend at school. Not until their teens do children tend to reject television. Then they tend to react against what they regard as one of their parents' home symbols. This rejection is in turn abandoned only a few years later with the curtailment of freedoms that comes with marriage, children and the economic pressures of rent or mortgage-payments. It can well be argued that all the world's a set, and all the men and women merely viewers.

The programme makers

As well as the NVALA and the politicians, a third group demanding change has now appeared – the programme makers. Broadcasting has evolved partly in response to the recommendations of a host of Committees and Commissions which the governments of the day have seen fit to implement by legislation. The report of the 1960 Committee on Broadcasting usually referred to as the *Pilkington Report*, was presented to the Conservative Government in June 1962. The condemnatory tone of this report reflected the beliefs of Professor Richard Hoggart, author of *The Uses of Literacy*, and a passionate believer in the values of working-class culture. He deplored the invasion of the British screen by an alien American culture, which is particularly intrusive on the ITV channels.

The recommendations of the Pilkington Committee startled many in the plush boardrooms of the 'big four'

ITV companies, ABC, Associated-Rediffusion, ATV and Granada. They were now faced with a Royal Commission's recommendation that their licences should be revoked and the responsibility for programming transferred to the ITA itself.

Down at the comfortable ITA headquarters in Knightsbridge there was consternation. Always the Cinderella of the ITV glamour stakes, they suddenly found themselves likely to be responsible for the programming of a whole network, if the Conservative Government accepted the Royal Commission's proposals. But there was never any real danger that the Conservatives would do this, since they had created ITV.

The national press, most of whom had shares in the ITV companies, reacted with hostility to the clear threat to the freedom and profitability of the programme contractors. So Pilkington was shelved, apparently indefinitely.

In the ranks of the producers and directors of the ITV companies much discussion ensued. If the programme contractors lost their licences, were their employees to lose their jobs, or to find they were employed by a new and unknown body, the ITA? Or, when the licences were reallocated in 1967, might some or all of the contractors be swept away and a new group appointed? The prospect of a programme company controlled by programme makers rather than by financiers was intoxicating. Few questioned the basic structure of ITV. The talk was all of reform, not revolution.

When the ITV licences came up for renewal in 1968, Sir Ivone Kirkpatrick, regarded by many as the great apologist and defender of the programme companies, had gone. His replacement, Lord Hill, former radio doctor and Cabinet Minister, did not accept that the existing programme companies were owed the automatic renewal of their contracts. Instead he looked favourably on the young groups of programme makers. In particular he was impressed by the consortium formed by compère David Frost and former Head of BBC 1, Michael Peacock; and by the Harlech group, formed by the former British ambassador in Washington, Lord Harlech, with *Panorama* reporter John Morgan and *Panorama* producer Robert Rowland, together with star names such as Richard Burton, Elizabeth Taylor and Stanley Baker. Rumour had it that both Paul Fox, subsequently Head of BBC 1 and now of Yorkshire Television, and Aubrey Singer, subsequently Head of BBC Features, would be future Controllers of Programmes if various other consortia were successful.

When the ITA appointments of programme contractors were announced, two of the old companies, Television Wales and West (TWW) and Associated-Rediffusion, had failed to win a licence. David Frost's group, London Weekend Television, and Lord Harlech's group (Harlech Television) won contracts. Telefusion won the new Yorkshire station, under the programme control of Donald Baverstock, former head of *Tonight* and BBC 1. It looked as if the programme makers were at last going to be allowed to have their say on the quality of programmes in the councils of ITV.

The promises made by the new consortia in their applications made exciting reading. In particular, Michael Peacock of London Weekend Television promised new miracles of quality programming daily. Alas, the new big four (ATV, Granada, Thames and Yorkshire) chose not to network all the LWT programmes on offer, with the result that LWT could not really afford to go on making quality programmes. LWT profits were unspectacular, so Peacock was dismissed. Six of his most talented programme makers, who had joined him at LWT from the BBC, chose to resign too. Their much-vaunted public affairs unit was completely disbanded, and its principal interviewer, Alan Watson, returned to the BBC. Protests by the press and other television producers about Peacock's dismissal by LWT were rejected by the ITA. LWT had not broken its agreement with the ITA, so there was little the ITA could do.

The Free Communications group of television producers grew out of the discontents of the years following the 1968 ITA shake-up. The Labour Government's levy on the gross receipts from television advertising hit many companies hard. Programme budgets were reduced, and producer discontentment mutiplied. Grumbles at having to pander to the lowest common denominator of taste became more shrill. An articulate programme of reform proposals was drawn up. Once it had seemed as if the ITA, in the person of Lord Hill, was not insensitive to producer demands. In the 1968 licence allocations his decisions had appeared to concede that programme makers made good programme controllers. But now Lord Hill was Chairman of the BBC, replaced at ITA by the former Labour minister Lord Aylestone, no great lover of change. The producers who resigned *en bloc* with Michael Peacock found themselves almost unemployable; the BBC was not going to buy back ITV casualties. Opposition to the existing mode, content and structure of broadcasting hardened, and two distinct types of producer-critic emerged.

The first group is the 'syndicalists' of the 76 Group (so called because the charters of both BBC and ITA were expected to expire in that year). They are totally opposed to the present structure of broadcasting, disliking the constitution as much as they do the present management. They believe that neither BBC-type bureaucracy nor commercial entertainment companies should monopolize and control access to television. They propose a range of alternative systems.[8]

The 'expansionists' are a very mixed group. They include independent producers, the Free Communications group, cable companies who want more 'wired' television, and those who simply want to collar the fourth channel, which is still to be allocated.

Many broadcasters believed that the Conservative Government would not allocate the fourth channel until after a Royal Commission had investigated the operation of British broadcasting, in the seventies. But the Conservative Government was not slow in allocating the licences for the new commercial radio stations, through the IBA. Then in March 1973 Sir John Eden, Minister of Posts and Telecommunications, cheerfully announced that he proposed to extend the licences of both the BBC and IBA until 1981, and that he hoped to allocate the fourth TV channel by 1974. But the Labour election victory in the spring of 1974 led to the re-appointment of the Annan Committee, whose report is awaited.

Optimistic 'expansionists' believe that some agency of the State should own and maintain studio and transmission equipment, making both freely available to any recognized body that wants to produce its own quality programmes. The fourth channel is ideally suited for such an experiment, which, if successful, could then be extended to the other channels. Pessimists feel that probably the present ITV companies will win exclusive access to the fourth channel, thus preserving the present situation where the programme maker is constrained by the profit motive.

Chapter Two

The Birth of 'Auntie'

The era from the accession of Reith to the arrival of commercial television spans forty years. During that time radio in Britain grew from a few low-power transmissions received by primitive crystal sets to a pattern of complex multi-waveband radio broadcasting, together with a fast-growing television network with twelve million licence-holders. For John Reith in 1926 the task of broadcasting was clear. It was to inform, to educate and to entertain.

But for Sir Robert Fraser of the Independent Television Authority in 1966 the task of broadcasting was to provide the kind of programmes that were acceptable to the largest number of people. The ITA should not worry if such a policy meant that the programmes did not rise above the lowest common denominator of public taste. 'This is free television in a free country and people will get the television they want, as they get the press and the government they want.' [1] It took over forty years for this more permissive attitude to evolve, and it embodied the antithesis of those values that John Reith held dear.

Reith's reign

How did so strange and so British a body as the BBC ever come into existence? After the First World War various enthusiasts began to listen-in to random broadcasts from various radio manufacturers. The British Broadcasting Company was formed from an amalgamation of these interests. On 13 March 1922 this company placed an advertisement in the *Morning Post* inviting applications for the post of General Manager. A 28-year-old Scottish engineering manager saw the advertisement, applied, was interviewed and accepted.

So it was that John Reith, a Presbyterian teetotaller, with the total conviction that God had destined him for this work, took over the creation of a broadcasting service for Britain. He saw his task in almost biblical terms. Broadcasting was to be 'a drawn sword parting the darkness of ignorance'. He believed passionately that in order to fulfil this ideal there should be only one broadcasting service, independent of the State, and free from the need to make profits. The company's dividend was limited to $7\frac{1}{2}$ per cent per annum.

In January 1927 the British Broadcasting Company became the British Broadcasting Corporation, an independent government-sponsored corporation, controlled by a board of governors who were accountable to the Postmaster-General. Day-to-day control was vested in the Director-General, who was in Reith's day a very powerful figure indeed.

How was such a corporation to be financed? The solution chosen was an inspired one. Instead of being paid for out of general taxation, the corporation would receive a fee derived from the sale of licences to every household with a broadcast receiving set.

Reith was intimately concerned with the creation of programming policy. What material was or was not suitable for broadcasting was of great concern to him. The *BBC Handbook* for 1928 explained that the BBC had to consider 'the unwilling audience, the people who if the matter were, say, performed in a hall, would not be there'. Therefore items which could be performed in a theatre or published in a newspaper were often considered unsuitable for Reith's BBC. In this he anticipated the view of Mrs Whitehouse by forty years.

One big development in programming was the emergence of a predictable programme-pattern each week. In the twenties programmes did not usually occupy the same time-slot each week. Today programme series appear at the same time each week in an utterly predictable flow, and the alternatives on other radio and television channels are equally predictable. Today audiences feel they have the right to expect certain characteristics from programmes they select. If they are disappointed or disgusted by what they see they have the freedom to change to another programme, or to switch off. In Reith's day this sort of choice did not exist. I agree with the television critic Peter Black when he writes of those people in the National Viewers' and Listeners' Association who made a point of watching series like the BBC *Wednesday Plays*, which seldom failed to shock them, that 'they placed themselves in a position in which nobody could do much to help them'.[2]

Broadcasting spread quickly in Britain for three reasons: it was interesting, it was country-wide and it was cheap. By September 1925 forty million people were in 'uninterrupted service' range of a BBC station broadcasting some six and a half hours each day. The number of ten shilling licences issued was about a million. It was estimated that over five times that number of wireless sets were in use. A BBC radio set cost between £2 and £4, which was no small sum in those days. Many people manufactured their own wirelesses from kits, at a fraction of the cost.

The broad policy laid down by Reith was to cater for the majority for about 75 per cent of the time. All programmes of national importance, no matter how dull, were broadcast between 9.00 p.m. and 10.00 p.m. However the choice in programming widened every year. By 1928 talks, concerts, children's programmes, outside broadcasts, religious services, light entertainment (rigorously purified of any risqué jokes) and educational programmes were finding audiences which never dropped below one million listeners, and sometimes reached fifteen million. Reith described his policy as concerned to 'offer the public something better than it now thinks it likes'.

The 1928 *BBC Review* summed up this general philosophy when describing the BBC music policy . . . 'Literally millions of people have heard for the first time in their lives the simple, youthful and sparkling tunes of Papa Hadyn; or the elegant Mozart and joyful early quartets of

Beethoven and realized that therein lies a wealth of melody undreamed of. Hosts of bright, impressionable children whose music has consisted mainly of snatches of music-hall ditties inflicted by itinerant executants in the bar entrance, or sobs of the worst type of sentimental slop played in the local cinema at the weekly popular Saturday performance, have heard over the broadcast such music as must have had a great and good influence on the sensitive unfolding mind.' Broadcasting was there to do you good, and no one questioned such idealism.

Over the next ten years, 1928–1938, the BBC steadily expanded its range of programmes and its general appeal. Although the statement on BBC musical policy quoted above undoubtedly held true for the million who enjoyed Haydn and Beethoven, several million others preferred the enormously popular dance-band leaders and their music. 'The Orpheans' from The Savoy, Ted Brown from the *Café de Paris*, Ambrose at The Mayfair and Jack Payne at The Cecil all became household names. Jack Payne began the BBC's own dance orchestra, and when he resigned to make more money elsewhere, he was succeeded by a man who survived into the seventies, Henry Hall, and his famous 'guest night'.

Radio drama made a promising start with some extremely talented writers of its own creation. Lance Sieveking's *Kaleidoscope* and Tyrone Guthrie's *The Flowers are not for You to Pick* were masterpieces of their time. Special features like the radio scrapbooks and the royal broadcasts widened the scope of radio. *Children's Hour* and light entertainment shows became enormously popular.

Only the news lagged behind. It was hampered by the restrictive practices of the newspapers, which succeeded in preventing the BBC from broadcasting news bulletins before 7.00 p.m. and giving live coverage of other events. But slowly the restrictions were lifted. By 1927 sporting events could be covered live, and by 1933 the news bulletins grew from twenty minutes to forty-five minutes in length. The BBC became a popular national institution. Only on Sundays did its puritan conscience sound loud enough to scare away the audience.

To many people the BBC Sunday was extremely boring. Reith believed he was guardian of the Sabbath – a jolly Sunday's broadcasting was no part of his plans. He wrote later, 'The surrender of the principles of Sunday observance is fraught with danger; even if the Sabbath was made for man the secularizing of the day is one of the most significant and unfortunate trends of modern life. Apart from any puritanical nonsense the Sabbath should be one of the inviolable assets of our existence; quiet islands on the tossing sea of life. The programmes that are broadcast on a Sunday are therefore framed with the day itself in mind.'[3]

Reith was convinced that broadcast religious services were of great value not only to the godly but also to those men and women who would never darken a church door if they could avoid it. 'There are tens of thousands who would not go to any sort of church but to whom are now brought the influence of a straightforward and manly religion. I know that even the singing of once familiar hymns has brought back the remembrance of happier and better days. There is no telling the effect when, for this brief period in a busy week, the lamps are lit before the Lord and the message and music of eternity move through the infinities of the ether.'

Reith's kind of Sunday broadcasting eventually resulted in increasing popularity for the commercial alternatives to the BBC. There were millions who wanted to escape from a diet of Bach's St Matthew Passion, Sheridan's *The Rivals*, classical music, *Heroes of the Free Churches*, *Treasures of the Bible*, *How to read an Epistle*, and the first of three half-hour talks by Canon Charles Raven on 'The Way to God'. (All of these programmes were broadcast on a single Sunday in April 1935.) Faced by such a diet, millions tuned to the continental radio stations – Radio Luxembourg, Radio Fécamp, Radio Toulouse and even Radio Athlone in Eire. Radio Luxembourg's audience was estimated to be between four and six million. The others probably only reached a quarter of that total. In 1936 spending by big British firms on radio-advertising of drugs, cosmetics and foods was estimated by the Institute of Incorporated Practitioners in Advertising to be in excess of one and a half million pounds. By 1937 the BBC had lost half its Sunday audience. It lightened its Sunday programme-content, reacting in the same way as it was to react to a far more serious commercial challenge twenty years later.

The BBC strenuously opposed commercial broadcasting from the Continent. It argued that such programmes undermined the programme standards of the public service, and that Radio Luxembourg had 'pirated' a wavelength not assigned to it by the International Telecommunication Union. Successive British governments tried by all the usual means to discourage these sponsored programmes, which featured nothing more harmful than popular music, some light drama and a number of American revivalist preachers who were not to be heard on the BBC. The programmes were popular, and the existence of wireless relay companies, which offered relatively interference-free reception for BBC and commercial stations at the flick of a switch, was to play a significant part in the demand for commercial broadcasting in Britain after the war. But in the thirties the various governments were determined to protect the BBC's monopoly.

When in February 1938 Sir Robert Boothby asked the Foreign Secretary about sponsored programmes from abroad, Anthony Eden replied that His Majesty's Government was determined to prevent commercial broadcasting to the United Kingdom from any source. However, the exercise of diplomatic pressure, currency regulation and even lobbying at the International Wavelength conferences produced little result. Only the outbreak of war brought the end of commercial radio for a few years.

The close of the thirties saw the end of the Reith era. Times had changed. Europe was on the brink of a holocaust, and the simple faith of a Scottish Presbyterian seemed to some to be increasingly irrelevant to the new generation. Had he wished to, Reith could have spent

several more years commanding the BBC. He chose otherwise, and surprised many both inside and outside the
Corporation by resigning in March 1938. As he walked
through the great doors of Broadcasting House for the last
time he was in tears. (He came to think later that his
resignation was the biggest mistake of his life.)

His achievement, with his colleagues in the BBC, was
truly remarkable. It is perhaps summarized best in his
own words: 'It was in fact the combination of public service motive, sense of moral obligation, assured finance, and
the brute force of monopoly which enabled the BBC to
make of broadcasting what no other country in the world
has made of it.'

The War years

Many people look back with nostalgia to that time of
national unity during the War when packed public houses
could be struck dumb listening to Churchill's voice crack-
ling through the speaker. Maurice Gorham, one of the
senior BBC men at the time, was not alone in feeling that
the War was a good thing for the development of broadcasting in Britain. For the first time the Corporation considered how to appeal to the masses and not just to the
educated middle class. In doing this it suddenly acquired
a witty common touch seldom discernible in Reithian
times.

The governors offered the wartime control of the BBC
back to the government, which wisely let the team get on
with the job – perhaps adding that one of broadcasting's
first tasks was to keep the nation cheerful. In this task the
broadcasters were magnificent, and none better at it than
Tommy Handley and the *ITMA* team. Their characters,
and indeed their phrases, have passed into English popular
culture: Mrs Mopp, Sam Scram and Funf. 'After you,
Claud. After you, Cecil!' 'It's me noives.' 'Can I do you
now, Sir?' 'I don't mind if I do.' 'Smile, please. Watch the
birdie!' 'Ah, there you are!' and 'TTFN' (Ta Ta For Now)
– to which Handley's memorable reply was 'NKABTYSI-
RWU' (Never Kiss a Baby Till You're Sure It's Right Way

Up). Puns and catchphrases made a real contribution to the nation's morale. The show rested on a huge fund of common knowledge. *ITMA* belonged to Britain, to everyone from the girls at the factory to the men at the front.

Other programmes touched a more serious note. An intellectual trio composed of Julian Huxley, Professor Cyril Joad and Commander A. B. Campbell brought intellectual discussion to an unparalleled popularity in *The Brains Trust*. Broadcast again in 1972 during the BBC's fiftieth anniversary celebrations, the programme seemed to have lost nothing of its brilliance. In the political sphere, J. B. Priestley made some memorable broadcasts full of imagery and insight in the *Postscripts*. His talks developed the theme that the War must be won in order to build a better Britain, not just in order to return to the old one. As pre-war Britain had been generally ruled by Conservative governments, the Conservative press turned openly hostile. The programmes were taken off, giving an interesting example of that fortunately rare phenomenon in British broadcasting – political censorship. Four years later the War ended, and political opinion swung very much the way Priestley had suggested it might.

Changes in broadcast political thinking were matched by changes in broadcast religious thinking. Dorothy L. Sayers' dramatized version of the life of Christ, entitled *The Man Born to be King*, was really revolutionary at the time. The Secretary of the Lord's Day Observance Society went as far as to publish an advertisement warning the nation against the danger of provoking Almighty God at such a serious moment in our history by what he saw as an irreverent, vulgar and blasphemous account of Christ's life. But neither the Almighty nor the BBC Religious Advisory Committee decided to object. Many people were struck as never before by the powerful drama.

The War years saw the BBC become less accent-conscious, and less male-dominated. Wilfred Pickles read the news, and women such as Joy Worth and Joan Griffiths became continuity announcers, something Reith would not have permitted in the thirties. Gone too was the

Reithian Sunday, torpedoed by the second service, the so-called Forces Programme. Throughout the War the Forces Programme was consistently more cheerful, less solemn than the other service. After the War the Light Programme took over where the Forces Programme left off. There was no return to Reithian solemnity.

Television overtakes radio

The BBC had begun the first high-definition television service in the world in 1936. Three years later, with 20,000 viewers, in the opinion of Gerald Cock, the first director of the television service, it had reached take-off point. Certainly the infant service had accomplished all those feats we now take for granted – such as outside broadcasts from Lords and Wimbledon; the Derby, the Boat Race and Promenade Concerts from the Queen's Hall. It had covered Chamberlain's return from Munich – and *Twelfth Night* with Michael Redgrave and Peggy Ashcroft from the Phoenix Theatre. In the primitive studios at Alexandra Palace, John Piper had talked about art, and Bernard Shaw had talked about himself.

Closed by the War, the service reopened in 1946 with an outside broadcast of the June victory parade. The evening's entertainment included Margot Fonteyn dancing, a variety show, a play and Bernard Shaw's *Dark Lady of the Sonnets*. It is perhaps a comment on our times that no Director of Television would dare put on so culturally-orientated an evening's programmes today, even on BBC 2, without more light relief.

Post-war television, like early radio, affirmed the Reithian belief that the BBC's job was 'to offer the public something better than it now thinks it likes'. Mary Adams wrote in the 1948 *BBC Annual Report*, 'The great majority of viewers like plays best, respond to first-class variety shows, enjoy magazine programmes and sport, accept without enthusiasm the more serious studio demonstrations and discussions, and dislike being educated or lectured at from the screen on any subject whatever. Contrary to belief, most viewers do not belong to the surtax class. The set, once bought, is installed in the most comfortable room, and widely used by the family as a whole.'

However, most viewers unconsciously shared the BBC's belief that television was an instrument of power and wonder, and that the duty of responsible broadcasters was to nourish and expand the viewer's range of taste. If not surtax-payers, most set owners were comfortably off, and delighted that they could afford moving pictures in the sitting-room. How many other toys would keep the children quiet in the afternoons and amuse the grown-ups in the evening? They knew no other kind of television. If one-quarter of the time was devoted to outside broadcasts, and a whole evening devoted to Glyndebourne, who were they to complain? The BBC's television audience liked the output, because, like them, it was comfortably middle class.

The event that really brought television into the lime-light was the 1953 Coronation. After some dispute with the authorities, permission was given to fill the Abbey with a vast array of television cameras and cables. The resulting visuals were magnificent, but what made the whole event so memorable was the sustained narrative-flow of the man destined to become Britain's greatest broadcaster, Richard Dimbleby. His feeling for an occasion was unmatched. The public enjoyed sharing his awe of ritual and royalty, and warmed to his treatment of the Coronation as an event of mystical, national importance. For the first time a television audience exceeded a radio audience for a national event and the stream of people ordering sets became a torrent, with 449,260 licence holders. Television had begun to reach the mass audience, and would be unable to remain in a cosy creative world of its own, safely insulated from the non-cultural demands of the uneducated.

There were many critics, yet as long as the BBC retained the 'brute force of monopoly' it could afford to shrug them off. 'Should one of the main events on Monday night have been the cooking of whitebait?' asked the *Daily Express* television critic, George Campey, in June 1951. 'Should the longest item on Wednesday be a film about the dairy industry?' (The BBC finally silenced Campey in the most

effective way possible – they made him their press officer.)
After a whole evening devoted to a re-creation of the
Elizabethan Age, complete with Shakespeare and Sir
Walter Raleigh giving a press conference, the *Daily
Express* led with the headline 'Twee Vee'. A large number
of viewers phoned in their complaints in strong terms.
They pointed out that they had not spent all this money
on buying a television simply to watch a sort of evening
class.

There were other, more powerful, critics of the BBC in
the background. 'Why,' asked the British Institute of
Practitioners in Advertising in 1946, 'should there not be
broadcast advertising?' As this prohibition was ordered by
the State, the onus of proving that this ban was desirable
lay with those who maintained it. The pre-war report of
the Ullswater Committee had stated that 'the intellectual
and ethical integrity of broadcasting should be maintained'. This, claimed the Institute, sprang from an unconscious dislike of commerce. As for fears of blasphemy,
swear-words and jokes about physical matters being introduced by commercial interests, BIPA claimed that advertisers would be far stricter about such matters than the
BBC, since they would never dare to offend their target
audience, the family. (The subsequent caution of the ITV
companies has shown this to be true.) What the Institute
wanted was for the BBC to be developed into a Post Office-
controlled system financed by private enterprise. At the
time, the Labour Government was hostile to any changes
for the BBC, and postponed holding any enquiry for five
years.

When the promised enquiry into the BBC opened in
1949, there were several pressure groups hostile to the
BBC's monopoly. These included the Fabians, the Liberals
and, most notably, the Chairman of the Commission himself, Lord Beveridge. The *Beveridge Report* rejected the
BBC's arguments that its past achievement entitled it to be
preserved unaltered. It rejected the claim that only a
monopoly organization could have high standards and
social purpose. It argued that the BBC was too big and too

powerful in relation to its artists. It asked how a monopoly could be free of complacency, injustice and favouritism. But after all this criticism it rather surprisingly concluded that the BBC should retain its monopoly position, without the introduction of advertising.

This conclusion carried less weight than it might because of a lengthy minority report submitted by Mr Selwyn Lloyd MP. In his view, the control and development of such a powerful medium of information, education and entertainment should not be left to monopoly control. Such a system led to the evils of unwieldy size, hindrance to technical developments, and the excessive power of a single employer. Though the BBC should continue to control radio, Selwyn Lloyd argued strongly that television should be financed by sponsored advertising, under the control of a British Television Corporation.

Published in June 1951, in the last days of a struggling Labour administration, its contents would have been welcomed by the government had they not been preoccupied by other troubles. Ernest Bevin was given the job of preparing a new charter for the BBC that would have enshrined in law the strength of its monopoly position for a further ten years. But he died suddenly, and discussions about peripheral issues such as regional commissioners dragged on for a further six months. Parliament was prorogued for the summer recess and in October Attlee went to the country. The result of the election was to be of critical importance for the whole future of British broadcasting, for Labour's majority of six became a Conservative majority of seventeen. The days of the BBC's monopoly were numbered. The critics now had the power and the will to attack both Beveridge and the BBC.

Chapter Three

The Populists versus the Elitists

The circumstances surrounding the arrival of commercial television in Britain make a fascinating study for historians, politicians, sociologists and moralists alike. Some, like Professor H. H. Wilson, see its arrival as the result of the work of a powerful pressure group operating within the Conservative Party.[1]

Sociologists postulate that some of the profound changes in society which occurred in the fifties and sixties have been influenced and accelerated by the advent of commercial broadcasting and by the changes towards more popular programming introduced by the BBC as a result. Broadcasters see the advent of ITV both as producing a competitive employment situation for themselves and as a move towards mass-audience television as we know it today.

All of these views contain elements of the truth. My own opinion is that the birth of commercial television was primarily a political victory by an important section of the Conservative Party, which was allied to powerful commercial forces who saw a real opportunity for profitable expansion. Politics and business frequently go hand in hand. Against such a combination the forces of the churches, the educationalists and the majority of MPs on both sides of the House proved surprisingly weak. While many people claim that the 'Establishment' is always on the side of the BBC, such a claim depends on who is regarded as being part of the Establishment. In this instance most of the Establishment were in agreement with Sir Winston Churchill, who as Prime Minister was not prepared to fight for a monopolist cause and for an institution which provided no profits for anyone.

The attack on the monopoly

The first political move against the BBC monopoly following the Conservative victory at the polls was the formation of a Conservative Broadcasting Study Group. Its membership included Ian Orr-Ewing (now Baron Orr-Ewing) a former BBC employee, John Rodgers MP, a director of Britain's largest advertising agency, J. Walter Thompson, and John Profumo MP, an ardent anti-monopolist. The Study Group produced a pamphlet entitled *The Future of British Broadcasting*, which saw this future as one freed from the allegedly undemocratic nature of the BBC monopoly.

The writers claimed that there was a real risk of an extremist government making the BBC an instrument of socialist propaganda. At the same time they attacked the BBC for what they alleged was its over-centralization, bureaucracy and rigidity. They argued that if Britain continued to deny choice in broadcasting there would be the danger of unauthorized commercial broadcasting from Eire or the Continent. With more enthusiasm than accuracy, the group made the astonishing claim that 95 per cent of Conservative backbenchers questioned the wisdom of allowing the BBC monopoly to continue.

In May 1952 the Conservative Government published their proposals for the future of British broadcasting. Their document took pains to reassure the nation that there was no intention to abolish the BBC. It conceded that the BBC 'had become an important part of the structure of our National life'. It went on to explain that the new charter would give the BBC another ten years to continue on the same basis, with greater freedom to begin capital investment. But the pamphlet continued by saying that the government had decided that 'in the expanding field of television, provision should be made to admit some element of competition'.

No specific proposals were made, but enough had been implied to enrage Lord Reith. In the House of Lords debate that followed, he reacted powerfully to the threat on 'his' BBC's monopoly position. Part of the debate had a Cromwellian flavour: 'Someone introduced Christianity into England, and someone introduced smallpox, bubonic plague and the Black Death. Somebody is minded now to introduce sponsored broadcasting.' Reith continued, 'Need we be ashamed of moral values or of intellectual and ethical objectives? It is these that are here and now at stake.' Speaking for the government, Lord de la Warr, the Postmaster-General, felt it was a 'conflict of negatives . . . it is really a case of deciding whether our dislike of monopoly is stronger or weaker than our dislike of sponsored or commercial broadcasting'.

Most of the speakers in the Lords supported the retention of the BBC's monopoly, but in the Commons many of the younger Conservative backbenchers felt that John Profumo spoke for them when he attacked the BBC's supporters for being self-interested. He claimed that of the BBC's supporters the Labour Party had a socialistic dislike of competition, the press feared a fall in advertising revenue, and the educationalists were contemptuously dismissed with the words 'we are not a nation of intellectuals'.

From May 1952 to November 1953 the rights and wrongs of the BBC's monopoly position were hotly argued by politicians, industrialists, clergy and teachers. The vast mass of the British public were not interested, and the arguments seemed remote and irrelevant.

Outside the Houses of Parliament the commercial television lobby was led by a powerful triumvirate consisting of Norman Collins, Sir Robert Renwick, who held fourteen directorships in the electricity supply industry, and C. O. Stanley, Chairman and Managing Director of Pye, the electronics company. They were helped by Mark Chapman-Walker, head of research at the Conservative Central Office, and later head of the ITV contracting company TWW (Television Wales and West).

Chapman-Walker came up with a clever modification of the American-style sponsored television programmes plan favoured by John Profumo and his lobby. Instead he suggested a State authority which would control independent commercial stations. These stations would produce their own programmes and recoup the cost by selling time to advertisers. He thus invented a classic British compromise, destined to be adopted by his party as a neat escape from the problems created by American-style sponsorship. His views were published in April 1953 in a skilful little leaflet entitled *Television – the Viewer and the Advertiser*. Enough safeguards were suggested to please the most sensitive of viewers and the phrase 'commercial television' was nowhere to be found. It seemed that the commercial lobby were riding high.

In June 1953 the preservationists rallied. At first, luck favoured their cause. It was generally agreed that BBC Television handled the Coronation superbly. Ninety-eight per cent of the twenty million who saw it on television said they thought the BBC had done a good job. Two days later, in a letter to *The Times,* Establishment heavyweights including Lady Violet Bonham-Carter, Lords Brand, Halifax and Waverley, and TUC Chairman Tom O'Brien argued that the future of television called for exercise of the highest sense of social responsibility. They urged the government to 'yield no further to the intense pressure to which they have been subjected, by a comparatively small number of interested parties'. The right course, they felt, was for the government and the nation to remain true to those principles that had made British broadcasting the finest in the world.

In the very same issue of *The Times* were reports and comment on the fact that those wicked commercial fellows in America had interrupted the televised recording of the Coronation service with advertisements for Willys cars ('the Queen of the road'). The *Daily Express*, always an enemy of ITV until it became a shareholder in 1968, encouraged the British lion to roar patriotically at the antics of a mere Yankee chimpanzee called J. Fred Muggs. Apparently during a broadcast in America the commentator had asked the chimp whether there were queens and coronations in the monkey world. Clearly this was the sort of behaviour the British public too could expect from commercial television.

The newly formed National Television Council found support for its aims flooding in from many disinterested religious and educational sources. It also received useful help from an interested party, the Associated British Picture Corporation, who saw how dangerous commercial television could be to the cinema industry. But apart from the loan of a public relations man, ABPC never appears to have provided financial support. After three months campaigning the total income from donations amounted to a mere £840.

How different was the birth of the Popular Television Association at St Stephen's Club, on 23 July. At the Turf Club a week earlier Lord Derby had graciously agreed to become the Association's President. It was a decision that was later to bring him more money than all his racing ever earned him. He was offered a major shareholding in TWW in grateful thanks for his support. Besides Lord Derby, the assembled company consisted of the two key members of the Conservative Broadcasting Group, Sir Robert Renwick and Mr C. O. Stanley of Pye. It remained for them to provide their new brainchild with a birthday present. The sum of £20,000 was immediately promised.

With so much money, their new baby grew up into a talkative child indeed, bombarding the media with Popular Television Association propaganda. Fourteen hundred newspapers and journals were flooded with a wealth of feature material. The PTA public relations man, a Mr Sims, became a brilliant and copious writer to the press in support of 'competitive television', as he liked to call it. Letters signed variously M. Awan, M. A. Warr, M. Adam, M. Swann, M. Ardan, all with the same address, appeared in at least twenty-two papers. A mythical Labour supporter called Leonard London wrote in support of competitive television to nineteen different papers, using the address of a secretarial bureau in Vauxhall Bridge Road. Mr Sims then proved what an observant fellow he was by writing to *Advertisers' Weekly* telling them he had 'noticed in the past few weeks a tremendous increase in the number of letters . . . putting the case of people who genuinely desire to have alternative services'. The honest men and women at the National Television Council, ably led by Christopher Mayhew MP, simply lacked the guile to compete against such methods.

By November it became clear that the Conservative Government had accepted the message of the Popular Television Association. Conservative MPs like Mr John Rodgers, who would have nothing to do with the Popular Television Association because it 'was set up by vested interests', were in the minority. The government's *Memorandum on Broadcasting Policy* embodied without change many of the proposals put forward in the advertising industy's pamphlet *The Viewer and the Advertiser*. There was to be no sponsorship. Programme content was to be the exclusive responsibility of the television station operator, not the advertiser. These station operators would be commercial concerns, who would make their profits by selling air-time. The actual transmitters and the over-all control of the alternative television channel would lie in the hands of a new government corporation set up to operate for ten years under a renewable charter.

The Bill to create the Independent Television Corporation was introduced on 4 March 1954. It provided for a grant of three-quarters of a million pounds to be paid to the new body, which would then administer the new system. Such government control outraged some Conservatives; the solution that had been reached was essentially a compromise, and sponsorship was avoided. During the committee stage no less than 206 amendments were tabled. In spite of this, the Bill became law on 30 July.

The Popular Television Association had won a great victory. But their manner of doing so has been questioned. Professor H. H. Wilson wrote, 'The whole campaign reflects the public relations stress on manipulation, the use of "gimmicks" to sell a pre-packaged policy.' Lord Hailsham called the bill a 'shoddy and squalid constitutional error' and attacked the government for 'deliberate concealment'.

Others, such as Lord Reith, thought the problems of introducing advertising into a whole new sphere of British life were only just beginning. For advertising must affect values and the concept of what is generally considered to be the good life. It is not merely the direct influence of the advertising message itself that is important, but the whole tone of programme content and orientation. Even without sponsorship, the majority of programmes tend to convey with varying degrees of subtlety, that life poses no serious problems.

Within ten years the Conservatives were to put out a party political broadcast that portrayed the whole of the country's future in the guise of a television commercial. 'Life is better under the Conservatives' – and this better life was shown to consist of a new house, well-dressed children and a new car. Conservative thinking capitalized on the commercial exploitation of consumer goods through commercial television. The materialism of the acquisitive society became a useful bulwark ... 'Don't let Labour ruin it.'

Two decades later we can see that the seeds of materialism produced more tares than wheat. If for many years people have been subjected to constant exhortations to 'buy, buy, buy', they will not take kindly to a sudden request for restraint. Richard Rose wrote that 'because the Conservative Party is so largely identified with the *status quo*, it cannot help but be benefited indirectly and almost accidentally by the insistent presentation to the electorate of stories and programmes which in one way or another make the point "things are going fine; there is nothing to complain about. If you have problems, change yourself, not society". The Labour Party suffers from independent television because it requires a widespread sense of social discontent to gain more votes.' [2]

It would perhaps be fitting to end this part of the chapter with a comment from an unlikely source, the leading Conservative thinker and writer, Peregrine Worsthorne. In the *Daily Telegraph* he attacked the 'hucksters who were asked to attract the crowds, but who have taken over the show.

"Give the people what they want" seems to have become not a means to an end, but an end in itself.'

'All that glitters . . .'

Sir Kenneth Clark (now Lord Clark, Chairman of the Arts Council) was appointed the first Chairman of the new Independent Television Authority. Clark is a most cultivated man, whose brilliant television series *Civilization* was years later to thrill many. His appointment was matched by that of Sir Robert Fraser as Director-General. Formerly a left-wing journalist and director of the Central Office of Information, Fraser brought with him an enthusiasm for making popular television in the cause of commerce that some found surprising.

Fraser's most difficult task was to implement the Act's requirement to 'secure adequate competition to supply programmes between a number of programme contractors independent of each other as to finance and control'. To do that adequately Fraser would have needed two rival stations in each area. To transmit their output he would have needed all eight channels on the VHF band – he had been allocated only two.

His solution set the pattern for ITV companies. Each station was appointed with a local monopoly. Four stations were appointed immediately, and the total eventually reached fourteen. The country was divided up into areas awarded on a points system based on the local population figures. The first four contracts were awarded to: Associated-Rediffusion (A-R) for London area weekdays; Associated Television (ATV) for midland weekdays and London weekends; Granada for northern weekdays; and the Kemsley-Winnick Group for northern and midland weekends. Kemsley-Winnick were unable to go ahead, and were promptly replaced by the Associated British Picture Corporation, which had previously helped the National Television Council to oppose the introduction of ITV.

Though Director-General of the Independent Television Authority, Fraser quickly realized that his power to affect programme content could only be used in a nega-

TRADIO TIMES

I.T.A.

SPONSOR SHALL SPEAK PIECE BETWEEN PROGRAMMES

CIGARETTES

RULES

"We see before us a new golden age. Are we to meet its challenge? It is not enough to ensure prosperity for the few; we must ensure it for the many: not enough to sell to those who do want; we must sell to those who don't. To-day there is no reason, if we are men enough, why the humblest in our great nation should not be choked with good things."—Mr. R. A. Butler

tive way. He foresaw that the companies would aim at attracting a *Daily Mirror* type of audience, and said so. 'This is free television in a free country and people will get the television they want, as they get the press and the government they want.' So once he had appointed the programme contractors, that was the end of his real control.

With characteristic frankness he put it like this, 'The authority has one moment of supreme and lasting influence over programmes; when it decides who will produce them, and who will not. The authority sees them as partners to be trusted, not as agents to be instructed.' Far from competing with each other, the companies were to work closely with each other in order to survive. Networking provided the only economic way to survive; their real competitor was the BBC.

On 22 September 1955, to the flourish of Sir John Barbirolli's baton, the Hallé Orchestra played in the opening of the independent television channel. They began as they did not intend to go on. ATV undertook to provide unaided thirty-five hours of programming a week. They were to discover that programming costs were one million pounds in excess of the figure they had been led to expect. With only 100,000 sets in the London area equipped to receive ITV, television was not a particularly attractive prospect in terms of cost-per-thousand for the advertiser. By July 1956 ATV had lost nearly £3 million. Alarmed at the sheer scale of the deficit, they sold 36 per cent of ATV shares to Cecil King of the *Daily Mirror* group for £410,000. As it happened, business picked up and they never needed the money.

The regional companies ABC and Granada opened later, and benefited from sharing programmes, a vital factor that reduced operating costs by 40 per cent in 1957. ABC lost £100,000 in its first year, Granada £176,000, while Associated-Rediffusion lost the princely sum of £2·7 million. Had they been forced into liquidation A-R's total liabilities would have been nearer £3·6 million. But A-R chose at this critical juncture to expand their holding by buying out the *Daily Mail*'s share, held by its parent company Associated Newspapers. A-R Chairman, Sir John Wills, bought the shares at 25 per cent discount from Lord Rothermere in a swift little deal after lunch at a farm in Sussex one weekend. Television stations, like so much else in our commercial world, had become saleable commodities.

Within two years profits from ITV stations looked good. ATV and A-R had made £2·7 million, with ABC a little behind with a modest £1·5 million. Only Granada had missed the millionaire class. Many people wondered why Granada's wily Sir Sidney Bernstein should lag behind. The answer lay in a secret deal between Bernstein and Sir John Wills of A-R, whereby A-R undertook to supply 85 per cent of all Granada's programmes, and to reimburse Granada for all its operating costs. In return Granada was to pay A-R the whole of its net annual advertising revenue less an agreed proportion. This resulted in Granada keeping a mere 10 per cent of the first million, and 12 per cent of the next three million. The unfavourable agreement terminated in 1960. In four years A-R had cleared a handsome £8 million.

Was the deal illegal? Certainly the secret deal prevented the ITA from fulfilling its statutory duty under the Act, Section 5(2). This states that the ITA must 'secure that there is adequate competition to supply programmes between a number of programme contractors independent of each other as to finance and control'. Not until 1961 did Bernstein own up to what could be construed as an evasion of the ITA rules (his confession appeared in the *Sunday Times*, 28 May 1961). Whether A-R and Granada were in breach of their contract remains uncertain. Some feel that morally they were. Certainly the ITA made conditions tougher when the rules came up for renewal, and A-R never got another contract.

ITV takes the audience

The ITV audience figures soared like a rocket. From 188,000 in September 1955 they rose to one and a half million by 1956, and reached over four million by the following year. By September 1957 Sir Kenneth Clark claimed that the public preferred ITV programmes by 79 points to 21 for the BBC. In that same year the Television Audience Measurement (TAM) ratings showed 539 ITV programmes against 3 BBC programmes in the Top Ten programmes for each week in the London area.

With engaging frankness Roland Gillette of Associated-Rediffusion announced, 'Let's face it once and for all. The public likes girls, wrestling, bright musicals, quiz shows and real life drama . . . we gave them the Hallé Orchestra, the Foreign Press Club, floodlit football and visits to the local fire station. Well we've learned. From now on, what the public wants it's going to get.'

How did the ITV companies achieve such a spectacular victory? Their most popular discoveries were the give-away quiz shows – Hughie Green's *Double Your Money* and Michael Miles' *Take Your Pick*. Associated-Rediffusion was never inhibited by the dictates of good taste and *People are Funny* depended on the crudest of practical jokes. Eventually the ITA got worried about the show and asked A-R to tone it down. But the company preferred to ditch it rather than dilute it.

If quiz shows were immensely popular, so were the variety shows produced by Jack Hylton for A-R under a special deal. Comedy and variety standards were often poor, but people love corny jokes, and the audience figures were always good.

By the autumn of 1956 the ITV network were running nineteen cut-price series and serials a week, including five on Saturdays. As Peter Black pointed out in his sympathetic account of ITV's early years, *The Mirror in the Corner*, these shows seemed to prove what the BBC had always denied, that most people needs must love the lowest when they see it . . . ITV seemed to be saying to the cultivated minority, 'We've won the mugs. Television is not for you. It is for them.'

Many of the ITV programmes were good by any critical standards. Some were far better than the equivalent BBC offerings of the day. Their drama was often superb. But it was in the field of news that the new channel really scored. Independent Television News – ITN – was produced by a non-profit independent company supported by the ITV programme contractors. The first editor of ITN, Geoffrey Cox, produced a new form of television star, the 'newscaster'. He hired two talented young reporters, Robin Day and Christopher Chataway, who were encouraged to provide a personalized view of the day's news. Both Day and Chataway spoke in a non-BBC style which was both more colloquial, and in a strange way more authoritative. It was certainly more entertaining. 'Personality', wrote Robin Day, 'should not detract from the news. It should give it added meaning and vitality.' Many felt that ITV current affairs programmes were more punchy than BBC current affairs. Devotees of *Tonight* and *Panorama* would not agree, but certainly the BBC had nothing quite like such programmes from the Granada stable as *Youth Wants to Know* and *Make Way for Tomorrow*.

Parliamentary and press pundits were less impressed with ITV popularity. Those who had remained in favour of the BBC monopoly reminded the public that they had been warned. Some of those who had supported the pro-ITV lobby felt aggrieved that their forecasts of independent television's good taste had proved to be mistaken.

The obvious scapegoats were the Chairman of the ITA, Sir Kenneth Clark, and the Managing Director, Sir Robert Fraser. Sir Kenneth remained optimistic. He admitted to the *New Statesman*: 'One has to swallow one's pride. You have to get a public first. Then you can build programmes of lasting value.' His one attempt to remedy the situation failed when the government turned down his request for half the £750,000 the ITA was entitled to spend on making its own programmes. Clark's plan had been to make a prestige current-affairs series. After its refusal, the government relented and offered him £100,000. But by that stage the companies realized that programmes from the ITA supported by public funds were a direct challenge to their individual area monopolies. They turned against the idea, and the ITA withdrew its request for government money.

Prelude to Pilkington

Every good general knows that the price of losing too many battles is the loss of his command. Similarly every politician knows that what is lost on the battlefield may be recaptured at the conference table. There was no doubt that the BBC had been heavily defeated by ITV. But it took time for the extent of the disaster to penetrate through the upper echelons of Broadcasting House. Several BBC 'generals' were to be replaced, and several BBC 'politicians' were to retire before the BBC won its great counter-attack, with the help of the Pilkington Committee on Broadcasting.

This committee was appointed on 13 July 1960 and published its *Report* two years later. Among its members were Joyce Grenfell, Professor Newark and Richard Hoggart, whose book *The Uses of Literacy* reveals how important he considers working-class culture to be. For Hoggart the choice was clear; was the Committee to support the BBC, which with all its failings made a serious attempt to preserve and develop British culture – or was it to favour the mass of American-orientated material shown by ITV?

This choice was crucial, because the Pilkington Committee had one rich prize to offer, namely the allocation of a third channel. Whichever contender won this channel would be in a strong position to attack its rival, by offering genuinely alternative programming. But whereas ITV could hardly afford to put on programmes for a small minority, and so would have to provide reasonably popular programmes on both channels, the BBC's position was quite different. With a second channel, the BBC could afford to place the bulk of its minority programmes on the second service, and thus be free to compete with ITV on its own terms on its first channel. In the fifties no such possibility had existed.

The man who had to face the attack from ITV, as Director-General of the BBC, was Sir Ian Jacob, a soldier by profession who rose to be a general and Military Assistant Secretary to the War Cabinet 1939–1946. He was quite clear what public broadcasting ought to be: 'It is a compound of a system of control, an attitude of mind, and an aim, which if successfully achieved, results in a service which cannot be given by any other means . . . The system of control is full independence, or the maximum degree of independence that parliament will accord. The attitude of mind is an intelligent one, capable of attracting to the service the highest quality of character and intellect. The aim is to give the best and most comprehensive service of broadcasting to the public that is possible.' (From a BBC internal paper.)

Appointed in 1954, Jacob foresaw that ITV would have a bigger audience, but believed that the BBC's good programmes would hold 40 per cent of the viewers, and recapture the majority audience for Christmas and Cup Finals. His Director of Television was George Barnes, the man whose appointment in 1950 had caused the resignation of the then Head of Television, Norman Collins. Barnes was a cautious man. It was partly his fault that BBC television news was so poor (but partly that of the appallingly overcautious Head of News, Tahu Hole). Barnes and Hole had to go. With the audience ratio in the summer of 1957 standing at 27 for the BBC as against 73 for ITV, drastic change was essential.

Morale was sagging. In spite of good programmes like the weekly *Panorama*, the fortnightly *Monitor*, plus *Tonight*, *Sportsview* and *World Theatre*, the great British public preferred pre-digested situation-comedy, and quiz shows such as *Double Your Money*. Not that BBC light entertainment was bad. The incomparable *Hancock's Half Hour*, *Whacko!* with Jimmy Edwards, the *Benny Hill Show* and the *Billy Cotton Band Show* all retained their admirers. The new Director of Television Gerald Beadle, promised that in five years he would restore the viewing ratio to 40: 60 without sacrificing BBC standards.

Good programmes are not the only ingredients necessary for success. What the BBC needed next was a superb tactician who could use programme scheduling to compete effectively. McGivern seemed to have lost his touch as a programme controller. Like Reith, he could never agree simply to give the public what it wanted; and like Reith he believed passionately that the public would respond to excellence. His beliefs had done much to shape BBC television since 1947. But it was time for him to move on, first to the powerless job of Deputy-director of BBC Television, and then briefly to Granada. But his heart was never in commercial television. He died in a fire shortly afterwards.

In appointing the former journalist and head of the Light Programme, Kenneth Adam, as McGivern's successor, the old general showed a shrewd grasp of the kind of man required. The signs of change were soon apparent. Gone was the hopeless BBC timekeeping, which compared so badly with the split-second timing of the ITV commercial breaks. Gone too was that advocate of a pre-war approach to news, Tahu Hole, the man who believed that bulletins must lead with items about the royal family, no matter how dull. In his place came a man with a genuinely fresh and anti-establishment viewpoint, Hugh Greene.

The talent was already there inside the BBC. Greene, as holder of the new post of Director of News and Current Affairs, gave the talent the chance it deserved. Huw Wheldon, Donald Baverstock, Michael Peacock, Paul Fox were all men who were to apply the lessons they learnt in the current affairs department to managing the war against ITV in the early sixties. Three of them were to go over to ITV at a later stage to collect the financial rewards the BBC can never give, and to lose some of the cultural rewards.

Hugh Greene was appointed Director-General in 1959. He was destined to exert as much influence on the shaping of the BBC as Reith himself. In many ways he was professionally far more qualified than any of his predecessors. During the War he had master-minded the BBC's broadcasts to Nazi Germany, and after the War helped plan the broadcasting structure of the new Federal Republic. As Head of the Psychological Warfare Department in Malaya during the emergency, he had charmed the communist resistance out of the jungle. Greene understood that propaganda by itself was not enough. It had to utilize the current situation to achieve policy objectives. Greene's policy objective was to win back the viewers, and to that end he began a skilful campaign to promote public support for the BBC. His first task was to win a second channel for the

BBC, arguing that a double-barrelled shot gun has twice the strike-power.

Mass-audience television had arrived. The BBC and ITV each wanted desperately to win the battle of the audience figures. For ITV they were the key to profits, for the BBC they might be the key to its whole future.

Chapter Four

Sold down the Sixties

The sixties were to bring three major developments in British television. First came the *Pilkington Report* in 1962.[1] This Royal Commission's findings were an undisguised attack on all that ITV had done, and its recommendations included a proposal to disenfranchise the contracting companies. Secondly came the birth of BBC 2 in 1964 and the growth of minority programmes, another Pilkington recommendation. Finally came the ITA's decision to change some of the ITV contracting companies in 1968 (and the subsequent failure of the new contractors to change much of anything). For BBC producers it was the intoxicating era of Hugh Greene – they really felt they mattered. For ITV producers, and those who joined them from the BBC in 1968, it was the era of the false spring. All that was promised in 1968, by programme contractors old and new, perished in the cold winds of economic recession.

The advertising bonanza

What was it about ITV that made the members of the Pilkington Committee react to it like members of the Mothers' Union threatened by the admission of the divorced and unmarried? Perhaps they were as much affronted by the unabashed commercialism of the advertisements as by the subtler materialistic mindlessness of many ITV programmes. They revealed no sympathy at all for the problems of an ITV programme planner – who could never afford to forget that his advertisers' object was to sell, which needed the constant attention of big audiences. Back in 1954 Sir Robert Fraser had been euphoric about the role that advertisers would play. 'Advertising will be an asset worn as a bright feather in the cap of free television, not as a soiled choker round the throat . . . I have sometimes wondered whether there could not be found some national cause, something deeper in the national life even than industry and commerce, to which the intelligence and conscience of advertising could be perfectly geared. Well, here it is.'[2]

The ITA rules about advertising content were certainly strict and there was to be no pressure by advertisers on programme makers. But hard commercial realities achieved the desired results, despite the rules. Successful advertising and successful programming had to be addressed to the same people.

Any fears that the public would reject the commercials were quickly dispelled. Market-research teams discovered that viewers had almost total recall of the early commercials, and that they continued to register them in their unconscious minds long after their conscious memories had faded. Whether they liked or disliked the commercial did not matter. All that the advertiser needed was that the viewer should react strongly. Once the brand name was firmly imprinted on the housewife's mind, it would automatically swim back as she stood bemused in front of the loaded supermarket shelves. The turnover from the television advertising industry grew from £17½ million to £100 million.

Typical of the runaway success enjoyed by many products in the early days was *Radox*, a footbath water softener sold mainly in the North and Midlands until television advertising arrived. Then in the autumn of 1957 its bright brand-manager decided to sell *Radox* not only for the feet but for the whole body. Endless filmlets showed happy people tiring themselves out by gardening, ironing, housecleaning and so on, only to be miraculously refreshed by a good warm bath in *Radox*. Four years later sales had risen 800 per cent. Is this a good thing? Moralists will differ in their verdicts; the Pilkington Committee seemed not entirely happy about the situation.

It can be held that there are two kinds of advertisements – those that inform, and those that persuade. Purely informational advertising amounts to only a small percentage of the whole. Apart from government advertisements to wear seat-belts, mind how you go and similar advice, few advertisers are concerned to tell you only what the product is for, or how it has been improved. The bulk of advertising is for competitive products like soap powder and petrol. Little can be made of their comparative value and merit. So what the advertisers actually sell is not the product itself but the connection between it and some quality the viewer would like to have – such as sex appeal, social one-upmanship, cheerfulness or good parenthood. They could also be described as selling pride, selfishness, sloth, covetousness, envy, greed and insecurity.

The IBA has endeavoured to control advertising excesses. They forbid false and misleading advertisements, disparaging references and political and religious advertising. For these restrictions we can feel grateful. But there are anomalies. Advertisers can suggest that all you need for a vigorous sex life is a particular brand of petrol; but you may not advertise any medicine, treatment or diet that offers a genuine chance of better performance in this field. Tobacco companies can advertise cigars, though not cigarettes; yet no commercial for a cure for smoking would be permitted.

How much faking is allowed to the advertising industry? Ice-cream, jellies and steam are difficult to film under the glare of powerful lights; white does not always look white on television. So under IBA rules jellies can be stiffened, and yellows and blues used to produce an effect of dazzling whiteness. Floor-cleaner advertisements appear to show grime removed from linoleum at a touch – but the substance you actually see removed is more likely to be soot.

ITV advertisers have also been responsible for spawning an unattractive breed of children who sell foods, soft-drinks and sweets. As long as these children do not do dangerous things or appear naked, they are fully permitted to eat and speak as badly as they choose. Such children occupy 20 per cent of advertising time, and can make a tidy sum out of their appearances. It is perhaps mere middle class prejudice to object to advertisers exploiting the emotions by using children.

Archie Graham of the Independent Television Code of Advertising Standards (ITCA) said: 'We have never taken the view that people need to be protected from romanticism and babies and puppy dogs.' However Jacqueline Wheldon in the television magazine *Contrast* (Autumn 1961) took a different view from Archie Graham. She considered that advertisers create unreal value standards. What they were really doing was to invite viewers to believe that the 'right' petrol and the 'right' washing-powder were matters of true social importance. She wrote: 'The way of living they invite us to aspire to is second-rate. They have turned their backs on the old, the slow, the difficult; their small powers of guilt are reserved for the presence of dirt and germs; their way of life includes no social arts, they sell standardisations at the lowest, common, quick and easiest level of taste, reaction and feeling.' She attacked the advertisers' prejudice 'against all the difficult decencies of birth, love, age and meaningful death; against the difficult slow decencies of real skills never seen, of anything that needs practice to make perfect, against the complexities of judgement, taste, goodness, endurance and learned toleranc, the complexities of the absence of these things; against tunes that aren't jiggy, joys and laughs that don't come instantly, cures that don't work quickly, against the value of pain and bad weather and discomfort; against the quality of life led by people who have learned to build into their own lives great griefs, and limitations of temperament and character.'

Peter Black, although often a defender of the ITV companies, summed it up well when he wrote: 'Although advertising's value is that it is the only method hitherto devised of financing television which interprets the public taste by box-office standards, a qualification is needed; what advertising does is to fix public taste at its lowest valuation, making it appear to be much lazier, more conservative and timid than it really is.' [3]

The materialistic undertones of commercial advertising are disturbing enough. But what about political and religious advertising? Should we feel thankful that it is forbidden? The American experience of political advertising has led to a vast increase in the cost of electioneering. Almost certainly in Britain the Labour Party could not afford to compete with the Conservatives if it had to pay the commercial rate for air-time. And the Liberals might find it hard to pay for even one broadcast. The present system of free allocation of air-time in proportion to the number of seats held by the major parties is surely much to be preferred.

The churches benefit in the same way by a free allocation of air-time to different denominations, worked out in cooperation with CRAC, the Central Religious Advisory Committee. By contrast, in the United States there are commercial 'plugs' for religious groups as well as sponsorship of complete religious programmes. Most people would agree that it would be undesirable if richer Christian sects could buy air-time, giving them an advantage over poorer sects. However, the IBA ban has its anomalies. One publisher could advertise a weekly part-work entitled *Man, Myth and Magic*, but another could not advertise a similar part-work entitled *The Bible Today*.

In spite of anomalies, Archie Graham of ITCA was confident. He argued: 'People have a fund of common sense that comes from their own experience. Society operates on this assumption.' Certainly the Conservatives, who are responsible for the introduction of both commercial television and commercial radio, would appear to believe this; and no political party, Conservative, Labour or Liberal, has so far sought to change the *status quo*.

Pilkington and the second channel

The Pilkington Committee's *Report* burst upon an astonished Fleet Street one autumn morning in September 1962. All that ITV's opponents had said against ITV now had the supporting weight of a Royal Commission. Judged by the standards of public service broadcasting, it was clear that the commercial companies had failed. As remedy, the Pilkington Committee suggested that the Independent Television Authority itself should sell the advertising, plan the programming and draw the programmes themselves from the existing contractors. (ITN had provided news programmes for the ITV companies on a not dissimilar system for some years. All companies paid levies for the news programmes out of their advertising income.) Now Pilkington suggested the ITA bought the programmes it wanted from the programme producing companies, but like ITN they were to have no access to advertising revenue. Most of the press immediately dismissed these plans as irrelevant or unworkable. Yet future inquiries (the Annan Committee for instance) could well reconsider them.

Pilkington suggested that the ideal ITA structure could be to divide Britain and Northern Ireland into television regions, each with its own executive appointed by the ITA to plan regional programmes. This executive could choose what national or regional output to transmit, having the opportunity to take other regions' material if he so chose. Under the present system, this very seldom happens. The regions either take their own low-budget material, or the output from the national networking committee. The big five pay scant attention to the smaller companies' desires. Pilkington suggested that the ITA's London Headquarters should plan the national network output and guarantee to take from the contractors a minimum number of programmes over a three-year period, providing it approved of them. Programmes would be planned by a joint committee of the ITA and the companies, who would compete to provide extra material for the Authority. For the advertiser, little would have changed, except that he would buy all his time from one source, the ITA, instead of from the different companies. (One boggles at the number of expense-account lunches that would be saved as a result; several Soho restaurants would probably go out of business overnight.)

The plan had many advantages over the present system, while retaining some of its best features. Programmes would still come from different companies, whose profits would depend on the quality of their output, not on the partly-accidental size of their area. The great disadvantage of the present ITV networking inflexibility would be overcome; programme men, rather than administrators, would choose programmes.

The ITV contracting companies and the national press (of whom all except the *Daily Express* owned a massive number of ITV shares) reacted with shrill horror to the Pilkington Committee's *Report*. Lord Thomson, owner of Scottish Television and *The Times*, reacted with a protest at such a 'completely biassed, socialistic and unrealistic report'. Peter Cadbury, a wealthy entrepreneur who owned Keith Prowse, the ticket agency, and Westward Television, gave a bonfire party at which he burnt a Pilkington effigy and six copies of the *Report* – a predictably non-rational response. The *Daily Mirror* commented: 'The Committee say you can't have the television programmes which a two-thirds majority of you prefer. You must have a different set-up controlled by the government: an "uncle" ITA just like "Auntie BBC".'

Over at the BBC in Portland Place, Hugh Greene was triumphant. He had won more than he had dared to hope – namely a second channel. Years later he wrote about the battle to gain this channel: 'The ITV, led by the old victors of the campaign for commercial television, made the usual mistake of thinking they were fighting the same war over again and were bound to win. They were lazy in the public presentation of their case, and fatally casual, even contemptuous, in the preparation of their evidence. They got what was coming to them.' [4]

The ITV companies did not get what was recommended for them. With the Conservatives, who had introduced commercial television, still in power, restriction of successful commercial companies was not to be expected. Very few of the Pilkington recommendations were implemented. Among those that were was the decision to abolish advertising magazine programmes like *Jim's Inn*. The ITA was given more power over scheduling.

Why did Pilkington support the BBC and attack ITV? Was it because Richard Hoggart was a fervent BBC supporter? Was it because the BBC in its evidence claimed that television had a vital effect on society, and claimed to be constantly aware of it, while Sir Ivone Kirkpatrick of the ITA thought that television was just one of many influences on society, and that society would change with or without it? Many theories have been advanced. One of the most credible is that the ITA had failed to guide the programme companies to produce quality in the way that the BBC had so ably guided its own output departments. The ITA was not wholly to blame for this situation. Perhaps if the powers that the Committee recommended be given to a reconstituted ITA had been given earlier, it would have solved some of the problems of controlling the companies' programme quality.

The Greene regime

Armed with the approval of Pilkington and a second chan-

nel, the BBC's most revolutionary Director-General set out
to change the 'Auntie' image. His first three years had been
spent in restoring morale, preparing for Pilkington, and
beginning to recapture some of the audience from ITV.
He was now armed with plenty of good programmes such
as *Look*, *Zoo Quest*, *Sportsview* and *Portraits of Power* as
well as such old favourites as *Panorama*, *Monitor* and the
drama and light entertainment output. The drama department's chief strength lay in three series: *Maigret*, *Dr
Finlay's Casebook* and *Mogul*. Its development of the
Wednesday Play was also successful.

Two new series were to make Hugh Greene's name
secure in the history of television. The first was the police
drama-series *Z Cars* and the second the current affairs late-
night satirical review *That Was the Week That Was*.
Many were outraged by the new image of 'Auntie'. That
the BBC should show policemen who wanted to know the
racing results, and who even knocked their wives about,
was a stunning change from *Dixon of Dock Green*, who
spent most of his time giving fatherly advice.

The undercurrent in *Z Cars* was one of social protest.
The series showed working-class Northerners who had
enough to eat, and more than enough to drink, but who
were starved of the graces of life and channelled their earnings into beer, bingo and betting shops. The *Z Cars* police
were no angels. They resembled tough, cynical sheepdogs.
The new realism paid off in audience figures as well as in
critical acclaim. Audiences rocketed from eight to fourteen
million. In vain did the Chief Constable of Lancashire
protest in anguish. Whatever the police and the Home
Office thought, *Z Cars* became a permanent part of BBC
drama output.

The late-night satire show *That Was the Week That
Was* on BBC 1 proved even more daring than *Z Cars*, but
much less permanent. By mocking everyone and everything, from seedy journalists to seedier politicians, it
earned itself the undeniable title of the most talked-about
show on television. Its ten million audience was treated to
jokes about all the subjects it was in bad taste to joke

about. The *TW3* team irrepressibly joked about religion and royalty, patriotism and protestantism, bull-fighting and fly-buttons. The Conservatives, as the party in power, came in for some savage send-ups. William Rushton's impersonations of the ageing Macmillan were magnificent. People took sides according to whether they were old or young, pro- or anti- the Establishment. The show was often uneven, and sometimes offensive. Much of the credit for its success went to a young Cambridge graduate and son of a Methodist minister called David Frost, but in fact the whole show was a team effort, brilliantly produced by Ned Sherrin. The politicians took more exception to the show than most people. A Conservative MP actually wanted to have the BBC impeached on the charge of holding up MPs to ridicule. Neither side relished the onslaught.

Sir Hugh Greene rightly took the credit for exposing what he felt to be one of the great cleavages in British society. He wrote later: 'It is of course a cleavage which has always existed; Cavalier versus Roundhead, Sir Toby Belch versus Malvolio or however you like to put it. But in these years was added to that the split between those who looked back to a largely imaginary golden age, to the imperial glories of Victorian England, and hated the present, and those who accepted the present and found it in many ways more attractive than the past. It was not a split between young and old or between Right and Left, or between those who favoured delicacy and those who favoured candour. It was something much more complicated than that, and if one could stand back for a bit as the brickbats flew, it provided a fascinating glimpse of the national mood. It also provided at times a rather distressing insight into the degree of sickness and insanity in our society.'[5]

The new Labour Government elected in 1964 showed itself as sensitive to satire as the Conservatives had been, although some of the sting was missing from *TW3*'s successor, *Not So Much A Programme, More A Way Of Life*. It substituted endless talk for the pithy comedy of *TW3*. The attempt to mix flippant clowning with serious comment did not really work. Milton Shulman, the *Evening Standard* television critic, summed it up in his usual testily perceptive manner: 'Commentators were selected because they were slick rather than wise, glib rather than articulate, indifferent rather than impartial.' After a furore created by a skit about a Catholic priest urging a Liverpool woman to have more children, the show was withdrawn in March 1965. The tradition of satirical shows was continued by *BBC3*, *The Late Show* and *The Eleventh Hour*, which often produced sharp and witty social comment. But the first savage impetus had been lost.

Any zest lost by the current affairs department responsible for the satire shows, was more than compensated for by the brilliant, original and some would say outrageous series of *Wednesday Plays* edited by the talented drama producer James McTaggart. He was determined that the Wednesday night spot should avoid being comfortable and conventional. In such Wednesday plays as *Cathy Come Home*, *Up the Junction* and *In Two Minds* – all produced by Tony Garnett and directed by Ken Loach – the BBC tackled difficult subjects like bad housing, abortion and schizophrenia in a new way. Blending videotape and film in a semi-documentary style, Ken Loach brilliantly re-created the sordid hopelessness of life for the submerged problem-cases of society. Though based on accurate social research, all these plays dealt with fictional characters, which led to charges of distortion and sensationalism. The National Viewers' and Listeners' Association (NVALA) took particular exception to the *Wednesday Play* series, and constantly complained to the BBC. Their protests were dismissed.

Even more outrageous to some were the two comedy series *Steptoe and Son* and *Till Death us do Part*. Steptoe was a sneering old man, usually at loggerheads with his assertive, day-dreaming, would-be-intellectual son, and their conversation was emphatically not the kind Mrs Whitehouse liked to hear in her drawing-room. The monstrous Alf Garnett of *Till Death us do Part* loyally supported God and the monarchy, the Tories and the family.

His racialist, reactionary sentiments allied with support for establishment causes was an even more devastating criticism of narrow establishment orthodoxy. In a remarkable way this East-ender yelling expletives and obscenities epitomized all that is intolerant, vicious and crude in the English character. Some Christians and monarchists were quick to deny that so vulgar and crude a man could possibly be on their side, but paid little attention to his layabout of an atheistic son-in-law whose arguments on behalf of intellectuals and workers were equally loaded.

Ian James of the *Catholic Herald* admirably summed up the results of the Greene regime when he wrote: 'While I regret and deplore the BBC's occasional lapses I also thank God for its courage. If the BBC was to play it safe, to confine itself only to cosy uncontroversial pap like *Coronation Street*, *The Black and White Minstrels* and quiz shows, it might have a peaceful time from the watchdogs, but it would be impossibly dull and unstimulating broadcasting. And it would also be failing in its duty to cater to all sections of the public . . . it is a positive duty for the BBC to put on programmes that occasionally shock, disturb and anger.'

Perhaps under Greene the BBC had gone too far for its own good. Harold Wilson was known to dislike his treatment at the hands of the BBC current affairs teams. Impishly he appointed Lord Hill, the former Conservative minister and head of the ITA, to the Chairmanship of the BBC Board of Governors in 1967. Lord Hill and Hugh Greene had their differences. Greene resigned as Director-General in March 1969. Lord Hill cannot have found it easy to work with a man with so much broader an approach to life than his own. With Greene's departure the BBC's irreverence seems to have departed too. The new Director-General, Sir Charles Curran, is more of a conformist defending a powerful empire.

BBC 1 had made all the running but the new BBC 2 had been slowly expanding since its inauguration in 1964. Michael Peacock, its controller, was at first convinced that every night of the week should have something different.

Sunday was to have opera, ballet and foreign films. Monday was to have light entertainment; Tuesday education; Wednesday repeats; Thursday minority programmes and hobbies; Friday drama and Saturday classic serials. The public, and more particularly the press, wrote off the second channel as strictly for the intellectuals. In fact most of them had never seen it, as it took time for people to buy new 625-line sets, and for the BBC to build the new transmitters. Audiences grew at a snail's pace, though the programmes were often good. I remember with particular pleasure the late James Mossman's contributions to the current affairs programmes *Encounter* and *Enquiry*. The lack of a large audience depressed him, and finally he returned to BBC 1. Michael Peacock's plan for different subjects on each night of the week failed, and was quietly dropped.

The following year Peacock went over to be Head of BBC 1, and the mild-mannered David Attenborough arrived to give BBC 2 viewers a feast of minority culture. Music flourished as never before. A whole evening was devoted to Klemperer conducting Beethoven's *Choral Symphony*, and another night to Benjamin Britten conducting his *War Requiem*. A brilliant twenty-six part series about the 1914–1918 war sewn together from library film raised angry complaints from those who could not receive BBC 2. A twenty-six part adaptation of the *Forsyte Saga* was equally popular with those lucky enough to receive it.

An important instrument of the BBC's success in regaining its half-share of the audience was its use of the technique known as 'time-junctions'. At first BBC 2 was exceptionally casual about timings, which seldom matched those of BBC 1. Attenborough soon made sure that there were at least three points when viewers had a genuine choice of programmes starting on BBC 1 or BBC 2. By and large the battle between BBC1 and ITV was between like and like, so BBC 2 usually offered a genuine alternative to both. The most successful coup in audience terms was the 8.00 p.m. time slot on Monday nights. While BBC 1 posed its current affairs programme *Panorama* against Granada's current affairs programme *World in Action*, BBC 2 gained an audience of up to five million for a quality western. By 1971 thirty-two million could watch BBC 2, and the habit of switching channels had spread.

Colour was another advantage to BBC 2. Introduced in 1969, it quickly spread to the other two channels. Colour enormously enhanced the BBC 2 minority programmes on golf, motoring, archaeology, finance, science, folk music, sociology, art, cinema and rugby league. Attenborough declared that 'the illusion that a minority programme is an intellectual programme is nonsense'.

BBC 2 provided some of the best programmes broadcast by the BBC in the sixties. Popular series came to be regularly exchanged between BBC 2 and BBC 1. Planned programmes and repeats on both channels made the BBC's position against ITV far stronger. It also led to renewed demands that a fourth channel should now be authorized by the Postmaster General, and given to ITV.

Chapter Five

The New Priesthood[1]

'The purpose of my remarks is to focus your
attention on this little group of men . . . who
wield a free hand in selecting, presenting and in-
terpreting the great issues in our nation. They
decide what forty to fifty million Americans will
learn of the day's events in the nation and the
world. We cannot measure their power and influence by the traditional domestic standards, for
these men can create national issues overnight.
They can make or break by their commentary a
moratorium on the war. They can elevate men
from obscurity to national prominence within a
week. They can reward some politicians with
national exposure, and ignore others . . . the
American people would rightly not tolerate this
concentration in government. Is it not fair and
relevant to question its concentration in the
hands of a tiny, enclosed fraternity of privileged
men elected by no one, and enjoying a monopoly
sanctioned and licensed by government?'
*Former US Vice-President Spiro T. Agnew
at DesMoines, Iowa, 13 November 1969*

When Spiro T. Agnew dropped his large rock into the
small pool of broadcasting opinion in 1969, letters received
by the broadcasting authorities supported his attack.
Twice as many agreed with him as those who disagreed. In
Britain there would probably be an equal number of those
from both Right and Left who would agree with Agnew
that the media are biassed, especially against theih own
party. Political points aside, what are the criteria by
which this 'tiny, enclosed fraternity of privileged men' act?
Are these criteria established by a range of individual

news-selection decisions, or is there some form of 'group-think' within broadcasting? Anthony Smith, a former editor of BBC's *24 Hours,* clearly thought there was when he wrote that broadcasting 'is a gigantic sluice through which all the currents of a nation's culture and current affairs are fed; it diverts them in its own interests and purifies them according to its own formula.'[2]

Factors in news selection

All the news contained in a half-hour news programme could be contained within just a couple of pages of a news-paper. Television news editors are 'gatekeepers among gatekeepers'. They have to exclude far more news than any newspaper editors are forced to. The main challenge to their journalistic skill is this need to exclude so much, which makes the task of selection all the more difficult.

The first factor that determines television news selection is the immediacy of the event. For an evening news broad-cast, what happened today is usable, what happened yester-day is probably stale. Communications satellites have made news from America and Japan available live in London, or relayed within hours of the event taking place. As a result, all news-editors tend to underplay the long-term background to events, preferring to present fresh developments. Coverage of running war situations, such as the Arab-Israeli conflict and the Ulster problem, tends to ignore the background which is assumed to be common knowledge to the viewer.

The second determining factor in news-selection is a geographical one, namely that the news story should be relevant to its audience. For example, a Birmingham strike is only a good national story if the strike has wide implications for the nation as a whole. Of all institutions, the government produces most news of national concern. Hence governments and their ministers will command a high proportion of television time, with a resultant built-in bias on the side of authority. This criterion of national interest also provides an inbuilt bias against foreign stories, especially if they involve the internal politics of another country, which can be difficult to explain in a few pithy sentences. The United States is an exception to this rule – British and European stations are exhaustively concerned with American problems, because film and tape are so easily available.

The third factor in news selection is continuity, or, as it is often called, topicality. If Belfast has been in the news, another bomb explosion is worth reporting. But on the other hand the public can get tired of a long war.

The fourth factor is that standby of all journalists, the 'folksiness' considered suitable for the mass audience. Children abducted by one or other parent to another country, dogs in space, and stories of humble heroism or amazing escapes all help to keep the viewers watching when decisive national and international events pall.

The fifth factor, one of the most important today, though ten years ago it was not considered so vital, is good visual material. This makes good television news, whether

"They're threatening to kill the story if they don't get a good zoom on a terrified hostage."

or not it features significant current events. Fires and fiestas, rituals and riots all make good television. Finally a good news telecast needs variety and pace. Some serious news and some light items will be included, even when all the important news falls solely into one category or another.

Television is a visual entertainment. A television news-editor who bores his audience simply ensures that his viewers switch over or switch off. So to every economic correspondent determined to try and explain the nation's troubles in a pithy five minutes, there is a news editor explaining that with luck the programme can spare him two and a half minutes maximum. (Non-visual subjects are doomed to suffer. The balance of payments and European unity are far harder to visualize than bombs in Belfast.) All six of these news factors are finally subject to the overriding need for split-second timing. News-editors have to produce the news at the right length at the right time. Speeches are cut to ribbons, key phrases omitted, and pictures so shortened that they appear only momentarily on the screen.

Criticism of television news coverage is usually confined to the choice of news values as determined by the selection of the lead stories. About once a month BBC Television news seems to wallow in sensationalism or unexpected trivia while weightier matters are relegated to a position later in the programme. Other more serious criticism has been levelled at BBC coverage of industrial disputes.

The Association of Cine and Television Technicians (ACTT) made a detailed study of news broadcasts in one week during January 1971. They concluded that: 'industrial affairs are covered in a superficial and haphazard fashion; that the BBC in particular scandalously failed to maintain impartiality in dealing with three issues during the week monitored; that ITV shows conscientious efforts to achieve impartiality; that unions may be partly at fault in failing to supply news and check its coverage'. There is some truth in the view that broadcasters echo the predominantly Right wing British press in presenting strikes as an anti-social activity on the part of workers, rather than as a result of a legitimate demand for higher wages which has been blocked by the employers or the government.

Minority groups often complain of television bias against them if their activities are not reported. Some sociologists now argue that there should be a conscious effort to democratize news. The American Professor Herbert Gans wrote: 'What I think we need is a pluralistic set of news media, which do not only reflect the predominantly middle class values of the journalistic profession, but also report the viewpoints, the events and the perspectives of every cultural and political group in the society, be they rich or poor, young or old, left or right, black or white, educated or uneducated.' The problem is that if such a series of news programmes were possible, it would not add up to the unified national news as we know it. The programmes would be more a kind of current affairs with a built-in bias, varied to suit the differing prejudices of the various groups, and would find only the already-converted prepared to switch on for the preaching.

The pattern of television newscasting imposes a framework that can lead to trivialization or bias, when the clock rules the editor's scissors. In current affairs television there may be far more scope for interpretation and the introduction of bias by personalities, but this is balanced by the need for the total credibility of the news.

Constructing current affairs programmes

Current affairs reporters and diectors have far greater flexibility than newsmen in working methods and approach. For programmes such the BBC's *Panorama, Tonight, The Money Programme* and *Europa*, and for ITV's *World in Action* and *This Week*, many of the constraints affecting news are not relevant. Absolute topicality need not apply. No news-peg is necessary for *Panorama* to conduct a major investigation into the social services. If such programmes do decide to do a piece on the Arab–Israeli conflict, there is usually time for an adequate resumé of the events leading up to the present situation.

Some reports are cameo portraits of a particular situation.

There are four categories of broadcaster among the 'New Priesthood' who work on programmes like *Panorama* and *This Week*. First is the reporter/interviewer. He it is who fronts the programme or the item within the programme, asks the questions, introduces and summarizes the story. He, or occasionally she, attempts to combine the dual roles of methodical journalist and tribune of the people. His status is in fact not that of a regular employee with pension rights, but that of a freelance journalist on short-term contract who may understand little about the art of television. While many reporters are very experienced, and have their contract renewed without question every year, the principle of easy removal remains, so that if a journalist offends political or industrial leaders, he can be removed hastily. Such a fate has befallen Michael Charlton in Australia with ABC, and (temporarily) Ludovic Kennedy with the BBC.

On location the film director and the researcher are equally important. The film director controls the camera crew and guides the reporter on his story. Sometimes the researcher ferrets out stories, and makes all the necessary contacts in advance. Many directors started as researchers.

Back at the studios is the final arbiter, the programme editor, the bishop who decides what mysteries may be shown to the millions of faithful worshippers at the cathode-ray tube shrines in countless homes. The programme editors are shadow men, unseen and unknown by the public, but whose word is final in cutting-room or studio rehearsals, and whose acolytes owe total loyalty, and who are usually sea-green incorruptible.

How do these four categories of the media-priesthood exercise their control of the electronic rite performed nightly or weekly for the electronic electorate? Here is the possible process of construction of a programme about that evergreen subject, the American multi-national company. The process is initiated by the researcher or director or both as they begin their research, usually based on news-cuttings, books and journalistic contacts. The subject is discussed with the delegated reporter, and the 'storyline' and its journalistic angle decided. The reporter would set out with questions like these: (1) Are the multi-nationals politically accountable to anyone? (2) Is United States investment in advanced technology in Europe inimical to the growth of European advanced technology? (3) Why should all control of American multi-nationals be from America, and their income benefit American shareholders only?

The next step is the decision about who and what to film, and where to go. Possibilities include IBM plants in France, the General Motors plant in Belgium, a United States bank in the City of London and an American drug company in Spain. Film of the various plants and of interviews with various members of the management and the workers is shot.

The third step is the editing. Many questions have been asked, but only a very few carefully-edited answers are used when the programme is cut to its final length, generally between ten and twenty minutes. When asking questions on location, the interviewer deliberately phrases them so that the answers from one man will be able to contrast neatly with the answers given by another interviewee. Talented interviewers use questions to relate the story for them according to a pre-determined storyline. The interviewee is usually unaware of this.

What the film fails to cover can be made up by the studio element of the story. The all-powerful programme editor, in discussion with the researcher, director and reporter, will decide how the studio element will be handled. Some editors are very dictatorial, some less concerned with detail than with the total impact. Possible studio guests for this fictitious item on the American multi-nationals are Jacques Servan-Schreiber, author of *Le Défi Américain*, and his contribution will probably be supplied from the Paris studio. Servan-Schreiber can be relied upon to attack the American multi-nationals vigorously. To balance him there will be a representative of an American multi-national, or alternatively a United States Republican congressman prepared to take the line that his country has provided both wealth and expertise through the United States multi-nationals. If a third speaker is required, who better to stoke the fires of controversy than that life-long critic of American big business, the American journalist Vance Packard, author of *The Hidden Persuaders*? If Vance Packard is not available, or the cost of a satellite-feed from a United States studio too expensive, then J. K. Galbraith, who is often in England, will be an equally positive and aggressive speaker.

By around 6.00 p.m. on the night of the programme the film sequences are ready, and the speakers are being briefed in lavishly-supplied programme hospitality suites. Sometimes the studio participants get the chance to see the film sequences before transmission, sometimes not. Anyone not in the studio, for example Servan-Schreiber in Paris, will only hear the soundtrack of the film without the picture. The film having finished the interviewer asks all three whether they agree with the various opinions expressed in the film, and battle commences. The interviewer in such a discussion plays a dual role. On the one hand he appears to be the chairman ensuring fair play; on the other hand he is also the interviewer posing hostile questions to both sides, and exposing points of dissension should the participants appear to be in danger of agreeing with each other. His aim is to open up the subject so that it is both interesting to the viewer, and controversial enough to divide his studio guests.

The sacrificial lambs

Our example points up some interesting attitudes on the part of the production team priesthood. Most obvious is their belief that it is incumbent on them to question big business. Bias is not unhealthy, providing you know it exists and can make allowance for it. What is to be questioned is bias shielded by the mask of impartiality. Anyone who agrees to participate should be forewarned that he does so at his own risk. How his case is presented is entirely in the hands of the producer.

The filmed interview is a bear-trap for the unwary. The

industrialist will have talked to the researcher or director in general terms before the programme begins, and on the basis of these discussions and other research he may then be filmed replying to some very leading questions about specific past events for which he is ill-prepared. Again, of ten questions he has replied to, perhaps part of only one answer may be used in the completed programme, and that one the answer most damaging to him.

Most film interviews take place in the executive's own office. In such familiar surroundings he may be led on to make damaging admissions he would never have made under the bright lights of a studio. Executives who leave interesting material littering their desk may find that their contents have been used in the programme. It took some time for big business in the United States to realize the threat to their activities posed by Ralph Nader and his associates. In the UK businessmen have been equally slow to realize that television reporters do not automatically accept the continued existence of the capitalist system in its present form as a good thing.

On location any rapport and understanding established between interviewer and speaker may help the interview. But the producer or programme editor is in no way bound by any conditions the interviewee may stipulate. Requests like 'You must use my last answer uncut' by the interviewee are usually refused, and even if the director were so unwise as to accept such a stipulation, the programme editor would not wish to honour it if he felt it compromised his journalistic freedom. Further, in order to make sure that there can be no retraction afterwards, the speaker is asked to sign a small slip of paper vesting all rights in his performance with the broadcasting company in return for a nominal performance fee, sometimes paid to an agreed charity. This 'blood chit', as it is called in the television world, effectively prevents the speaker from complaining afterwards that his interview was distorted by the editing process. Nor can he withdraw from the programme since he has already signed away all his rights in his own performance.

There is one further practice that can affect the balance of an interview. After he has been filmed answering the interviewer's questions, the camera is turned round on to the interviewer himself while he asks the same questions again, the so-called 'cutaways'. Though the producer's assistant repeats the questions back to him word for word, the interviewer may well be dissatisfied with a question that reads, 'In the light of the United States balance of payment crisis, and bearing in mind that American companies have been able to buy into European businesses at below their true values, would you not agree that there is a case for much higher taxation of American subsidiaries in Europe?' He might well shorten it to the more pithy question, 'Are American multi-nationals really evading the payment of their full tax contribution to European exchequers?' This is, of course, a different question, and though the motive for re-recording is one of professional pride, not malicious distortion, the effect upon the participant's case can be the same.

Choice of participants in studio interviews is also an area for subtle editorializing. BBC's *The Money Programme* once filmed an item about an American company in Scotland which did not permit unions because, they claimed, everyone was equal. After the film insert had shown that there were no separate offices in the factory and everyone used the same canteen, toilets and car park, the studio discussion began between the meek little American manager and Britain's most articulate and devastating white-collar union leader, Clive Jenkins. Whether you believe the American was right or wrong in his management methods, he never stood a chance in the ensuing discussion. Clive Jenkins had researched the whole background, and verbally destroyed the American, a destruction which the reporter in the studio did nothing to halt. However, it can be argued that on numerous occasions union leaders have themselves been effectively outgunned by highly articulate debaters, since the language of the Trade Union meeting is very unlike the language of television debate.

The New Priesthood seeks to maintain impartiality and most of its members are fair-minded individuals. But being so articulate they find it difficult to cover up their own usually radical beliefs. To go back to the sample programme, there has not been to my knowledge a programme which dispassionately evaluated the multi-nationals' contribution to European progress. Trevor Philpott might claim to have done so, but like many British journalists of his generation, his journalistic flair comes before any attempt to make the informed economic assessment for which his training did not prepare him. American multinationals are a perfect television Aunt Sally. The television audience has a chance to indulge its latent anti-Americanism, and to anaesthetize those nagging doubts that British is no longer best. The New Priesthood know this; they seldom show any reluctance to tell the worshippers what they want to hear. Such a programme is weighted from the start and the questions are angled in such a way that the audience are programmed to react unfavourably.

Television journalism and natural justice

When it comes to investigative journalism, members of the New Priesthood have to tread a delicate path between the law and natural justice. In British television today, as perhaps in British society, there exists a liberal consensus, and those who stray beyond its limits, with or without breaking the law, are legitimate targets for criticism and condemnation. The laws of libel inhibit some comment, but also inhibit comment which might imply criticism of the law itself. The BBC issued no retraction and apology for the accusations made by the former *Panorama* reporter Michael Barratt when he chased the property racketeer de Freitas down a street in Notting Hill Gate shouting questions. But they did show themselves more sensitive over the 'Hanratty' case. When Jeremy Isaacs was editor of *Panorama* back in 1965–66 he chose to mount an interesting programme querying the guilt of an Irishman called Hanratty who was executed for a shooting which came to be popularly called the 'A6 Murder'. During an interview with a man who knew an unusual amount of generally undisclosed detail about the case, the camera panned most suggestively down to the subject's hands. The programme then came to the conclusion that reasonable doubt existed as to who had perpetrated the murder, and whether the right man had been hanged. This may or may not have been a faultless conclusion but the programme openly attacked a legal verdict.

Sometimes a television interview leads to a High Court writ, which effectively and unfortunately stifles further comment by both press and television. A good example is the remarkable interview by Brian Widlake of the International Investors Group financier Jerry Hoffman in the summer of 1971 on *The Money Programme*. During the course of this interview Hoffman was asked why he had been banned from trading on the New York Exchange. Then Widlake challenged Hoffman to state why he was a fit person to head up the International Investors Group, owning at it did the twin funds of the Real Estate Fund of America (REFA) and the Fund of the Seven Seas (FOSS). (Both these funds were illegal under American law, and could not be sold in the United States.) The two other directors were partners in a firm of London solicitors. Worried at the unfavourable publicity created for their company by *The Money Programme* interview they slapped a High Court writ on the BBC alleging slander. This prevented both the BBC and the press from publishing further details of what appeared to be a highly questionable financial operation. Within two months the Fund's expensive offices at the Thorn Building in St Martin's Lane were closed, and the staff dismissed. Hoffman fled to Rome, where the intrepid *World in Action* team tracked him down. Ignoring the High Court action they produced a magnificent programme which nailed Hoffman's IIG for the confidence trick it really was. They revealed how its funds had been transferred from the Bank of America to Bermuda, and from Bermuda to a Swiss bank purchased by Hoffman. Mysteriously this purchase was never completed and the money disappeared. High Court ban or not, ITV current affairs had dared to tell the truth when the BBC and the press had been effectively silenced by the High Court writ, issued by directors of the company at fault. Hoffman and his girlfriend fled to Yugoslavia where he was intercepted by the Yugoslav police, and then to the United States where he was promptly arrested and sentenced to two years imprisonment for the offences which Widlake had referred to when Hoffman appeared in *The Money Programme*.

I have recounted this incident at length, because it illustrates how television, like the press, can be the watchdog of our society, provided the law does not stop it barking. There are advantages as well as problems in giving members of the New Priesthood freedom to comment. But we must make the journalists clearly responsible as individuals for what they say, so that personal vision is not given the weight of impartiality. A free press and free broadcasting are two of the great checks to ensure justice in our society. In addition television should not be restricted to being the mouthpiece of a chosen few in the 'priesthood', for with exclusivity can come subjectivity.

Outside interests

Worn-out journalists have long taken refuge from the pressures of their trade by becoming public relations consultants. Unfortunately, successful current-affairs journalists do not always wait to leave television before collecting cheques for being television consultants. Cliff Michelmore, Michael Barratt, Alan Watson, Brian Widlake and many others have earned three-figure cheques for telling industrialists, bankers and others how to face the cameras.

The most famous instructor in the art is perhaps Stanley Hyland, former deputy head of BBC current affairs, and dubbed by the *New Statesman* 'Mr Golden Microphone in Waiting' for his work in polishing the Harold Wilson television image. His company, Hyvision, dispenses television advice to executives of such varied pillars of the community as the Imperial Tobacco Company and the Metro-

politan Police. His pupils are taught how to prepare for
and survive a television interview. Commendably, Hyvision makes no attempt to claim that it can influence television producers in their choice of interviewees. Stanley
Hyland is no longer part of the network television world,
though he retains some useful contacts.

However it may be undesirable that well-known television journalists whose integrity is trusted by the public
should seek to augment their incomes by accepting payments from industry for television-acclimatization interviews. Do such payments by industry to journalists create
an unrecognized but nonetheless real sense of obligation
in the journalist? The pupils must often hope that by
virtue of having parted with a three-figure sum they will be
asked to appear on television by those who trained them,
thus deriving valuable free air-time for their company.
Looked at in this light, £100 is cheap for a passport to free
television exposure. That those who have been trained are
seldom asked is beside the point. Clearly a man who has
been coached in a practice situation will be in an altered
relationship to the interviewer should they subsequently
meet in the live studio. Bacon claimed that the money
he was paid made no difference to his judgements. I have
heard a television reporter make the same claim: but such
possible restraints on the approach of an interviewer by
reason of previous financial relationships are to be deplored.

More serious for the public are those few, happily rare,
cases where a television reporter has accepted a large retainer from a big company for consultancy services. For
those in the know it was distasteful to see a leading political commentator for a Sunday newspaper conducting a
series of sycophantic television interviews with leading
industrialists. He was in receipt of a £3,000 retainer from
one of the great Anglo-Dutch multi-nationals at that time.
The final interview in the series was with the Head of this
particular multi-national. So he was in effect interviewing
his own paymaster.

Any television journalist should declare his interest to

his employer, who if he knew the connection would not employ the journalist for such a task. Ever since the 'payola' scandals in the United States, the major networks like NBC and CBS have checked out the backgrounds of their leading commentators. Reporters, like MPs, should be forced to register their outside interests. In particular, financial reporters and producers should register their shareholdings. How much wiser is the system employed by many merchant banks who insist on their employees surrendering the control of their own investments while they are working for those banks lest they be tempted to take decisions of more benefit to themselves than to their clients. Caesar's wife must be above suspicion.

The New Priesthood have both the opportunities and the temptations that great power confers. Their job depends on their resisting temptation. Those who transgress will be reprimanded and transferred or will have their contracts terminated. The public interest requires that those men and women on whom it depends for impartial television presentation of news and current affairs should be seen to be without fear or favour.

The impartiality of the broadcaster

The BBC has no precise code of journalistic practice. It trusts its producers and directors and the journalists who work for it on contract to maintain impartiality at all times. Where there is an area of doubt, it relies on its staff to refer problems upwards. Much attention has been paid to streamlining the internal processes of communication, particularly since the problems of the situation in Northern Ireland have made the job of reporting both sides of a dispute even more difficult. At the top, the Board of Governors meets fortnightly, and reserves part of each of its meetings for the discussion of recent programmes. The Director-General meets his Board of Management weekly, and they too spend part of their time discussing recent programmes. The actual day-to-day control is the responsibility of the Editor of News and Current Affairs and his senior editors who all meet the Director-General weekly.

In the words of a BBC memorandum: 'General guidance and particular rules of conduct flow down through directorate and departmental meetings to the editorial conferences at which immediate programme decisions are constantly being made. Ideally, this flow should be clear and uninterrupted, but in practice, of course, some channels occasionally get blocked.'

It is of course easier for administrators in the calm of their carpeted offices to take considered judgements than it is for producers and directors who spend most of their lives in frenetic activity on location or in studios. But it is not just a question of time – it is also the question of differentiating the role of a current affairs producer, a documentary producer and a journalist. The documentary producer has to be the midwife of opinions and ideas rather than the exponent of them, but his craft demands that such exposition be sufficient to make them clear. The borderline between impartial and partial exposition of ideas is very narrow, and leads to endless discussion. The BBC documentary group set out some of their ideas in an interesting document which said more about the problems involved than about their solutions. Describing the role of the producer in regard to the editorial initiative of his work it said:

'The producer or director of a documentary occupies a complex position. On the one hand he *is* the BBC; half of him cannot escape being an official delegated to supervise broadcasting policies and practices. On the other hand half of him has creative responsibilities to the programme. Since many programmes deal with matters of high controversy, the question is often asked: if a producer has very strong partisan views about the subject of this kind of programme (e.g. supposing he is producing a documentary about public schools, yet is himself violently against the independent school system) should he not allow his own views to dictate the nature of the programme? The classic answer is that unless he can lay his own views totally on one side, he should on no account be producing this particular programme at all. To express his views would be a total abuse of the powerful platform he controls. There are many people, including the Prime Minister, who are constantly denied access to such a platform, and just because a man happens to work for the BBC certainly gives him no right to it. If the producer still feels intent on expressing his views, he should leave the BBC and make his name in some other field. Perhaps one day he will be invited back in his own right to express his views as a contributor.'[3]

So the answer is clear for the staff employee, who in effect represents the BBC in its programme origination capacity; he must seek to remain impartial at all times. But most of those we see on the screen as reporters and investigators are not BBC staff members. They are journalists who have precise knowledge and opinions about many of the subjects they report. A programme presenter is often a man who has written books on the issues he is reporting on, and may in himself embody a known point of view. Yet he has to carry the weight of the BBC or ITV reputation for impartiality. Three principles were produced by the present Director-General, Sir Charles Curran, in consultation with the senior news and current affairs editors:

a. 'A good professional ought to be able to operate impeccably in areas about which he has strong personal views.'

b. 'When answering the question why, a Current Affairs man may start with a hypothesis but not with an evident commitment.'

c. 'Every time a man reveals a personal commitment he reduces his professional usefulness, until the moment arrives when he may be said to have used up all his credit-worthiness.'

The implications are quite clear. The BBC will continue to use freelance journalists and others on short-term contract so long as they do not reveal bias. Should they do so, they can expect a speedy end to their engagement.

'Bias' is capable of definition; 'balance' is harder to define. In recent years the question of balance has become more and more important, as stronger and stronger expressions of opinion are permitted, provided they are balanced by similarly outspoken comments from the alternative viewpoint. Only by balancing opinions can the BBC avoid the charge of editorializing. But to balance every expression of opinion can lead to colourless broadcasting. Sir William Haley, a former Director-General and subsequently editor of *The Times*, put it like this in 1945: 'Impartiality does not mean so artificially balancing speakers that the listeners can never come to a conclusion, on the basis of the argument.' Twenty-three years later Sir Hugh Greene summed up how thinking had moved away from balance within a single programme to balance within a series of programmes. He wrote: 'We have to balance different points of view in our programmes but not necessarily within each individual programme. Nothing is more stultifying than the Current Affairs programme in which all the opposing opinions cancel each other out. Sometimes one has to use that method but in general it makes for greater liveliness and impact if the balance can be achieved over a period, perhaps within a series of related programmes.' [4]

Broadcasting is an evolving art. The creeds of one generation are challenged by the next. Programmes like *The Family* would have been unthinkable ten years earlier. Producers and directors try to stretch their freedoms and their impact as far as they can. Sometimes they go too far. When that happens, the men at the top enunciate new doctrines to cover the new situation. Members of the New Priesthood have powers similar to those of the great preaching orders in the Middle Ages; they lead, and others follow. But like all members of an order, they show a remarkable ability to close ranks when criticized. This chapter, to the extent that it reveals some of the mysteries, may produce exactly that effect on reviewers and commentators. They will claim that it is exaggerated or unbalanced; the very charge of which they themselves stand accused.

Limitations and temptations

In May 1970 Robin Day, probably the best current affairs

interviewer alive today, put on paper his 'Troubled Reflections of a TV Journalist' (*Encounter*, May 1970). What he said produced sympathetic echoes in the minds of many television professionals throughout the business. It was remarkable not so much for its originality, but for the passion with which he stated his reflections. He saw the limitations which affect television journalism as being of two kinds – imposed and inherent. The imposed limitations I have dealt with earlier; the inherent limitations deserve further mention.

Day's first worry was the familiar one, that television depends far too much on newsworthy pictures. Far too many news bulletins were put together on the strength of the pictures rather than on a journalistic evaluation of their true significance – that remained the prerogative of the weightier newspapers. To combat this trend, Day argued for more reasoned debate, argument and exchange of ideas. To counter television's increasing concentration of action, usually violent, he wanted to see what the telly men call 'talking heads'. Always the champion of debate-style editions of *Panorama* rather than long film reports, he attacked those who spurn the 'talking heads' programme with a fine display of rhetoric. 'Talking Heads . . . In that contemptuous phrase, the image merchants of the electronic age dismiss the one characteristic of man that elevates him above the beast, the power to conceive and communicate rational thought. Man's supreme gift is seen in terms of what the eye sees on that wretched little screen: a talking head.'[5]

But Day's point is a valid one, and has been echoed by no less a commentator than Theodore H. White. White considered that the arrival of the thirty-minute coast-to-coast news programmes in the 1960s actually created the demand for dramatic pictures of conflict; the Civil Rights campaign produced nearly as many as the Vietnam war. In the reigns of Johnson and Nixon the American viewing public became increasingly like the crowds in the Colosseum in the reign of Nero, their appetites for battle and violence whetted by the diet fed them by the television broadcasters.

White spoke primarily of television journalists in the USA when he wrote the following, but the same could be said for British television journalists: 'One irrevocable cowardice binds all men in television – television dare not be dull. The logic is simple: if a television show is dull, then it loses its audience; if it loses its audience, it loses either sponsorship or executive protection; if it loses these the producer goes broke or is removed. Whether television feeds on excitement, breeds excitement or provokes excitement is a matter of intricate debate. Whatever the answer is, there can be no doubt that television spreads excitement, and that any producer, knowingly or not, recognizes that the law of his survival requires that he speed the spread.' [6]

The other great limitation of television is that of time. The parable within the television world tells of the news event when Moses came down from the mountain with the Ten Commandments to meet waiting newsmen.

'What do you have?' they asked in chorus.

'I have the Ten Commandments,' replied Moses.

'Tell us about them, but keep it to ninety seconds,' they said.

Later that night the story has become still more condensed, and the newscaster announces: 'Today at Mount Sinai, Moses showed up with Ten Commandments, the three most important being anti-sex, anti-homicide and an attack on the consumer society . . .'

Continue the parable and imagine the carefully-rigged audience for a Frost show, that travesty of serious current-affairs programming freely indulged in by both BBC and ITV. 'Tell me, Mr Moses, don't you feel that you have an essentially outdated view of the family in society . . .? We have in the studio one representative from Gay Lib and two from Women's Lib, besides Jerry Rubin, your supporters from the Jesus Freaks and the former Bishop of Woolwich.'

Part of the time the problem derives from programme-overcrowding, indulged in by experienced producers as well as the light-entertainment people who run the Frost shows. Overcrowding can arise from the perfectly laudable intention to cover a subject from several aspects, and to 'balance' opposing views. But compressing too much material into too short a time-slot often produces snippets of ill-digested information, so the programme becomes trivial where it should be comprehensive. Worse still an item designed to run thirty minutes can be cut to fifteen because of some news event. I remember with shame an item on the reform of Parliament which included thoughtful contributions from Professor Bernard Crick and Michael Foot, and which was shortened till it made comparative nonsense. An outraged Professor Crick swore never to take part in such a travesty again. He received an apology and a second fee, as if a distinguished academic could be bought off with a few guineas, when in fact important material on the subject of his life's study had been thrown away.

The destruction or distortion of material has worried many. Stanley Hyland, veteran producer and former assistant head of BBC Talks, once said that few subjects were so clear that current affairs could not muddy the issues. In February 1975 London Weekend current affairs producer John Birt wrote in *The Times*: 'There is a bias in television journalism. It is not against any particular party or point of view. It is a bias against understanding.'

But perhaps the most illuminating evidence of the deep concern among producers about the genii they have unloosed came in a letter to Robin Day from an experienced current affairs producer after he had read Day's 'Troubled Reflections'. 'If current affairs producers (and even more so news producers) don't take care they may lose control of the medium, which has a strong inherent momentum in the direction you indicate. Current affairs coverage could become so showbiz that it's a public disservice. Television should serve its material and not the other way round. It is the evening medium and for many people now, the only source of serious "current affairs" journalism. Producers

". . . and although no governments have recognised our declaration of independence, I'm happy to tell you we have aroused the interest of 'Panorama'."

must recognize that most important developments are not primarily visual, and should be treated at least as much in their own terms as in television's, if viewers are not to be misinformed and miseducated. It seems to me that it is very hard to inform, educate and entertain simultaneously. All too often, the result misinforms, miseducates and fails to entertain.'

Discontent with the limitations of the media is not confined to current affairs departments. In a sensational but secret document produced at Kensington House in the spring of 1976 and submitted to the Annan Committee, the BBC General Features department producers put their names to a long document attacking the whole of the present structure of control in BBC television. They felt the whole monolithic apparatus had become too vast, control was too remote, creativity was being stifled, and the men at the top were remote from the producers who set the tone. Huw Wheldon, then director of television, listened sympathetically and Alasdair Milne, Head of BBC

2, set up a working party to see how a series of smaller creative units could be built out of the monolithic, but cost-effective, organization. But rather as Parliament uses Royal Commissions to appear to be doing something while in fact doing nothing, so the BBC uses working parties to take the steam out of difficult situations.

What of the role of the interviewers and reporters? The late fifties and early sixties threw up a race of giants, men whose integrity and professionalism towers above the lightweight men and women who grace evening current affairs programmes in 1976. Among the giants I would cite Robin Day, Michael Charlton, Julian Pettifer, Brian Magee, and, those no longer with us, James Mossman and Kenneth Alsopp. The Dimblebys, father and sons, have kept the standards of integrity and impartiality high. All of these men have been eager to present reasoned and civilized argument which is part of the democratic process by which we are governed. By contrast David Frost has excelled on an appeal to the worst lynch-mob tactics of the hand-picked audience baying for blood, be the subject capital punishment (with big close-ups of the murdered person's close relative) or a cabinet minister (Denis Healey) very properly refusing to reveal defence secrets for the benefit of London Weekend Television.

Chapter Six

Television and Politics

'Yonder sits the Fourth Estate, more important
than them all.' *Edmund Burke, 1722*

'He who moulds public sentiment goes deeper
than he who enacts statutes or pronounces
decision.' *Abraham Lincoln, 1858*

'The primary function of radio and television, as
far as the political process is concerned, is to
confer fame and status.' *Anthony Smith*, The
Shadow in the Cave, *1974*

'In the television election, the Electorate sits down
to watch itself preparing to exercise its power
and is shown a rat in a cage.' *Trevor Pateman, 1974*

Politicians came to use television slowly and reluctantly.
Then times changed, and today politician and television
producer embrace each other with enthusiasm. Yet this enthusiasm is increasingly tinged with cynicism: neither has
benefited from the encounter as much as he would have
wished. The politician has had to adopt the style and
jargon of the entertainment world to be accepted by the
television audience. The television producer, always seeking profundities in sixty seconds, has found that political
truth is neither as easy or as dramatic as he would wish.
Political policies are often too abstract for good television,
so producers rely heavily on portraying politics in terms
of rival personalities.

Producers prefer verbal fisticuffs, and the fact that such
contests often produce more heat than light is less important than the fact that a good row results in good viewing
figures. As Richard Crossman, the late Labour Cabinet

Minister, said at the Granada Guildhall Lecture on 21 October 1968: 'The coverage of politics, outside the news bulletins, consists chiefly of interviews, arguments and confrontations between the spokesmen of the two parties which play up the gladiatorial aspects of politics, and give the impression that it consists of a mere conflict of personalities rather than a conflict of ideas carried on by personalities.'

Between the cat and rat games of the minister of the Crown versus the self-appointed tribune of the people, or the all-in wrestling of political prize-fighters, there is little to choose. The public may be entertained; they are seldom enlightened or instructed. This is not to say that there are never serious political programmes in Britain and America. Some political television has been superb, but it is usually insufficiently attractive to retain the interest of the mass audience, except in times of crisis.

Does television make performers of all politicians who appear? BBC *Panorama* reporter Robert MacNeil felt that it might: 'It can be argued that for the whole American nation, television has made the actor-politician inevitable. Television is indispensible to politicians, and the television audience is conditioned to like glamour and style. Therefore politicians become glamorous and stylish.' [1] There is also the fact that the medium can distort not only the nature of serious political debate, but also the contributions of those political leaders seriously involved in the political process. Some television producers would avow that it is healthy to show politicians as they really are, or as television shows them to be. Some producers delight in showing up the egotism, stupidity and pettiness of men in power. Others, faintly contemptuous of their unpaid performers, appear to feel that any minister should be accountable day by day for the work of his department, and should the poor man fail to produce the quick answer, or the impromptu joke, he will not be asked again.

It could be argued that television, in the way it treats politicians and political news, actually contributes to the disillusionment with the political process now being experienced both in the United States and Britain. It is worth examining political television in America in order to try and assess its influence on British politics on television today.

USA – television and the President

No president before Eisenhower seriously attempted a speech on television. Truman feared the medium, and refused to allow his press conferences to be televised. As for his predecessor, Roosevelt, the problem never arose. Indeed, it is interesting to speculate whether, if television had shown Roosevelt as he was, an invalid in a wheel chair, he would ever have been elected at all.

Eisenhower soon learnt the power of television, thanks to the dramatic come-back of his vice-presidential running mate, Richard Nixon. The details are worth recalling. During the course of the 1952 presidential campaign the press revealed that Nixon had accepted 18,235 dollars from seventy-six wealthy Californian Republicans. A vigorous campaign to get Nixon dropped from the Republican ticket soon got under way.

To defend his position Nixon went on television via 256 stations to tell his version of the incident – with the help of an advertising agency. Twenty-five million Americans heard Nixon rebut the 'slush-fund' charge. He went on to admit that he indeed received one gift of a political nature – a dog. He said in his familiar voice: 'A man down in Texas heard Pat on the radio mention the fact that our two youngsters would like to have a dog. And believe it or not, the day before we left on this campaign trip, we got a message from Union Station in Baltimore saying that they had a package for us. You know what it was? It was a little cocker spaniel dog in the crate that he sent all the way from Texas. Black and white spotted. And our little girl, Tricia, the six year old, named it Checkers. And, as you know, the kids love the dog, and I just want to say this right now, that regardless of what they say about it, we're gonna keep it.'

Given half-an-hour of television time to fill, Nixon did

go on to promise to drive 'crooks and communists out of Washington', and to praise his running mate Eisenhower. But what people remembered about his speech was the picture of Richard Nixon as Mr Ordinary American, complete with wife and daughters, talking on the screen about his debts, his mortgage and his dog. 'You're my boy,' said a delighted General Eisenhower, by then secure in the knowledge that, as requested, viewers had written in to the Republican Committee overwhelmingly endorsing Nixon as vice-presidential candidate.

Two sociologists Kurt and Gladys Engel Lang summed up the whole incident like this: 'While there was much criticism of Nixon's unscrupulous use of theatrics, his "soap opera" appeal, the low level of intelligence at which he had pitched his defence, and the use of show business methods in politics, no-one could deny that his political technique had been effective.' [2]

Nixon had found a new way of getting out of a political jam, by baring his heart in public. Later, Senator Edward Kennedy was to do the same after the death of Mary Jo Kopechne at Chappaquidick in July 1969. Kennedy could have made a statement, given a press conference or made a speech to the Senate. Instead he chose to speak to the people direct through the medium of the television confessional. The viewers were not to see the speechwriters, prompting devices and rehearsals that went into his performance. 'By God, he told the truth', said Senator Aitken of Vermont, on seeing Kennedy's broadcast, and millions agreed with him.

To return to Eisenhower, at the beginning of his presidency only one-third of the American public were exposed to television. In 1955 Eisenhower held his first televised press conference, which was subsequently heavily edited by his press secretary, James Hagerty. Even so, on the screen Eisenhower appeared long-winded, confused and rambling. Within a few months there was a transformation. The President now appeared natural and relaxed. How did he do it? 'The President had employed Robert Montgomery as a television consultant, and the actor had become the first show business personality with an office in the White House,' revealed Robert MacNeil.[3] Eisenhower ran into crises, as all Presidents tend to do. He was the first to use television to explain such varied pre-occupations as the state of his health, when seeking re-election in 1956, the Little Rock disturbances, and the warning to Maoist China to keep away from the Chinese Nationalist islands of Quemoy and Matsu.

By the time of the Kennedy era television had really arrived on the political scene. Many people finally decided to vote for Kennedy on the basis of the Kennedy-Nixon televised debates. Kennedy himself said, 'It was television more than anything else that turned the tide.' Once President, Kennedy introduced the 'live' televised press conference. Like Eisenhower, he appeared on the small screen at all times of national crisis – the Bay of Pigs incident, the Cuban missile crisis, school integration, steel industry rows and disagreements with Congress. But, all the same, he knew about the dangers of over-exposure, and never risked this in the way that his presidential successors did.

Lyndon Johnson was first seen as American President on British television making an 'I'm just a local boy'-type broadcast, which somewhat appalled the *Panorama* audience. Mischievously but understandably, the BBC had used the only film record of Johnson available, a homespun performance to his Texas electors, which was no help in enabling British viewers to evaluate the man so suddenly elevated to the White House. Once in the White House Johnson's television technique was suitably polished up. He began to speak faster to minimize the languid effects of his Southern drawl, and he exchanged his metal-rimmed glasses for contact lenses to give a less austere appearance. A television studio was installed in the White House, permanently kept on a five-minute stand-by, like the United States Air Force nuclear bomb force. With television so easily available to him, however, President Johnson soon fell into the trap of using it too often. He was for ever, it seemed, back on the screen, with a rather hang-dog expression explaining some fresh disaster, be it big-city violence, student riots, racial conflicts or the interminable troubles in Vietnam. 'Oh, there's Lyndon again; what's the trouble this time?' viewers began to respond.

Clever television packaging helped to give Richard Nixon his victory over Hubert Humphrey in 1968. He was determined not to repeat the mistakes he had made when he had been defeated by Kennedy back in 1960. There were to be no risky person-to-person debates. Instead a Madison Avenue agency with up to four million dollars to spend set out to sell Nixon like any other product, such as a car or a bar of soap. Market research was carried out to discover what was the American consumer's ideal for a president. Professional presentation on a whole series of expensive commercials portrayed the Republican presidential candidate as the genuine cellophane-wrapped ideal president. He became a kind of combination king, Pope, hero, father and male-lead. Above all he was an essentially nice-guy, skilled at his job. Since the actual issues were judged to be far too difficult to portray, the communicators concentrated on this aura of the essentially likeable and competent guy.

Nixon's sixty-second commercials were brilliant. Instead of showing the real, unlovely Nixon, they focussed on the problems of poverty, race, welfare and violence, while Nixon's voice as commentator intoned the expected clichés. William Gavin, one of Nixon's own staff, summed the effects up well when he wrote, 'What you leave unsaid becomes what the audience brings to it. Lead them to the brink of the idea, but don't push across the break. It's not the words, but the silences where the votes lie.'

Like Johnson, Nixon met a series of disasters in his first term of office. The real Richard Nixon now appeared, and with his disguises stripped he was seen to be a long-faced funny-looking guy frequently explaining the problems of his office, and very different from the master-figure implied in his campaign commercials. He always seemed to be announcing that he had a problem – the Cambodian invasion, the economy, the drugs problem and the race problem.

For those not devoted to their party leader, these endless catalogues of his failures and fallibilities left in the mind what television critic Milton Shulman has called 'negative residual'. He commented: 'Trust in the ability of the leader begins to ebb; suspicions about his confidence and even honesty begin to harden. A nugget of doubt is lodged in the viewer's mind and consciousness. This negative residual, left behind by a television appearance, is extremely hard to eradicate. Since the next time the leader appears on the small screen, once more asking for sympathy or support, over some depressing issue, the earlier scepticism about the President's ability to handle affairs is confirmed. The negative residuals accumulate with time, until a positive hostility or dangerous cynicism develops not only towards the leader but to the party and views he represents.'[4]

Besides the 'negative residual' a re-evaluation was at work, which added to the general disenchantment with Nixon. It became increasingly clear that the Nixon the television advertisements had spoken of, the 'king-Pope-hero-father-male-lead' Nixon, had never existed. The President they had elected was just the same 'would you buy a second-hand car from this man?' type that his opponents had always implied he was. So political advertising on television had secured the victory the Republican party supporters had paid for, but American democracy had suffered. The distinguished historian and politician, Arthur Schlesinger, described the selling of the President by television: 'This development can only have the worst possible effect in degrading the level and character of our political discourse. If it continues, the result will be the vulgarization of issues, the exaltation of the immediately ingratiating personality and in general an orgy of electronic demagogery. You cannot merchandise candidates like soap and hope to preserve a rational democracy.'[5]

Keenly aware that his Republican administration was up against these factors, Vice-President Spiro Agnew made a brilliant retaliatory strike at the media in his DesMoines speech of November 1969, by blaming television commentators for the administration's unpopularity. He cleverly implied that any objective or outside criticism of Nixon's speeches immediately after they had finished was not only unfair, but unworthy, undemocratic and unpatriotic. Referring to Nixon's Vietnam speech on 3 November, he said: 'When the President completed his address – an address incidentally that he spent weeks preparing – his words and policies were subject to instant analysis and querulous criticism. The audience of seventy million Americans gathered to hear the President of the United States was inherited by a small band of network commentators and self-appointed analysts, the majority of whom expressed in one way or another their hostility to what he had to say.' Within six months the commentaries had ceased to be critical. Far from showing up Nixon and Agnew for the arrogant and often incompetent men they really were, the news media toned down their criticism as a result of pressure from top management fearful of government action against them through the Federal Board of Communications. But the television networks' revenge was not long to be delayed.

In February 1972 Nixon was to pull off his biggest television coup of all, nicely timed to precede his election campaign. His visit to China became a vast television spectacular. As hosts, the Chinese leant over backwards to organize the whole programme for television coverage, since they were fully aware of the propaganda value of such coverage for themselves as well as for Nixon. It was in the interests of both sides to make the event a public relations triumph, and that is what it became. As Milton Shulman aptly described it: 'To achieve these diverse ends, both sides conspired to throw electronic dust into the eyes of the viewers, knowing that they had at their behest the finest instrument man has yet devised for fooling most of the people most of the time.'[6] What could any Democratic presidential candidate offer in face of such a public relations triumph? Nixon hardly needed to appear again in order to have impressed himself indelibly on his voters' minds throughout the electoral campaign.

Superficially his overwhelming victory in November 1972 seemed to prove his television success. Since his previous four years of office had built up 'negative residuals', because the Nixon image had not been able to stand up to such extensive television exposure, his advisers contented themselves with the extremely favourable viewing effects of the Chinese trip. For the rest of the campaign Nixon only gave two televised talks, which must have been the lowest number he could permit himself without giving the impression of being frightened to appear. Significantly he did permit himself thirteen radio talks, radio being a far less revealing medium. However, his election success was less that of the favourite, more that of the least unattractive, the least bad of the contenders for 61 per cent of the American people.

Senator Muskie might have been a far more serious rival to Nixon than George McGovern with his apocalyptic rhetoric, but Muskie lost the chance of the Democratic presidential nomination when he burst into tears in front of cameras because of a newspaper attack on his wife. Before the advent of television such an event might have passed unnoticed. Today a presidential candidate cannot afford to weep in front of the cameras without raising questions about his stability in a crisis. (It is instructive to recall that Winston Churchill wept to see the damage done to London during the blitz, but no cameras recorded the event, nor was he ever accused of weakness because of those tears.) Muskie did not receive the Democratic nomination. It has since been alleged that Nixon supporters engineered the whole incident in order to ensure that Nixon was faced by the weak McGovern, rather than by the resourceful Muskie. If this is true, then Nixon supporters were Machiavellian television manipulators indeed.

Newsweek, commenting on the Nixon victory, referred to 'the suspicion that his victory was a shallow one, built less on affection for him than on antipathy towards McGovern and his New Democrats'.[7] With only 54 per cent of the electors having troubled to vote, Nixon had done little more than prove himself less unpopular than

McGovern, on the lowest turnout in twenty-four years. The late Professor Sir Denis Brogan commented in *The Spectator* for 18 November 1972: 'People trusted his sense, including his sense of his own interests, more than they did George McGovern's sense of American or his own interests, but it was a very tepid support, and would not stand much wear and tear if things went wrong.'

Then came Watergate. The floodgates of pent-up hostility of press and television against the President were released. The fact that some of the Watergate hearings were televised simply added fuel to the fire. Television had helped to put Nixon where he was; television was now going to show just how vulnerable he really was. Columnists and television men had long had a genuine distrust of 'Tricky Dicky', a distrust which verged on distaste and dislike, and which he and his arrogant Press Secretary, Ziegler, entirely reciprocated. The White House's continual denials became less and less credited, and the culmination of media scepticism was fully vindicated in the spring of 1973 when Press Secretary Ziegler announced that some of the White House's previous denials had now become 'inoperative'.

'Increasingly it became clear that the Administration had conducted a massive campaign of deception to hide its actions and defame the press. It is clear from the tape transcripts that the President himself withheld evidence from the public. It has long been clear that his principal aides lied and lied again while accusing the press itself of lying.'[8]

Another press and television victory was the enforced resignation of Vice-President Agnew, the spearhead of the counter-attack on the media. All the past scepticism about the President and the Vice-President had been proved to have been justified. And the casualties? Not only Nixon and Agnew, but the methods of American democracy itself, its processes cheapened and vulgarized by the media, only to be betrayed by the beneficiaries of those processes, its own politicians. No more sobering conclusion about the effect of television on American politics can be quoted than that of the sociologists Kurt and Gladys Lang. Their evidence clearly reveals that television in the United States contributes to disillusionment with the political process. 'The media, we contend, can stir up in individuals defensive reactions by their emphasis on crisis and conflict in lieu of clarifying normal decision making processes. Thus, the individual's resistance to appeals for political support is often rationalized by disgust at the low state of political ethics.'[9]

Great Britain – television and the Prime Minister

The development of political television in the United Kingdom has not precisely followed the pattern established by the American networks. Mercifully political advertising time cannot be bought. Instead the main political parties are provided with a series of short slots by the broadcasting authorities free of charge. The two big parties receive an equal share while the third party, the Liberals, having far fewer seats in the House of Commons, receive a correspondingly smaller amount of air-time on radio and television.

'Party Political Broadcasts' as they are called vary from blatant copies of soap commercials (the Conservatives tried this in 1964, drawing many letters of protest in *The Times*) to serious one-man talks by the leader of the party concerned. Neither method is particularly successful in holding the audience, but often the broadcasts are transmitted simultaneously by both main channels, which gives little chance for the public to escape, unless they switch to the minority channel BBC 2 – and even that escape route is not always open to them. The studio facilities are provided free by BBC or the Independent companies; but film inserts have to be paid for. The Labour and Liberal Parties use the BBC facilities. The Conservatives feel more at home within the portals of profit-orientated transmission companies, and often make the whole programme on film in advance. As a result, their performances are often more polished, but less spontaneous.

The BBC usually offers to appoint a special television

adviser to each leader. In 1964 and 1966 Harold Wilson benefited from the ministrations of Stanley Hyland. In the 1966 election the Conservative leader, Edward Heath, who was considered inept on television, was given as his mentor David Webster, an ex-*Panorama* producer and Labour voter. Being essentially first an expert television man and only secondly a political animal, Webster did as good a job with Edward Heath as anyone could have achieved.

There are three types of political television broadcast usually seen in Britain, not including the news broadcasts. Perhaps the party political broadcasts are the least influential, but all three political parties insist on retaining them, as being the only programmes over which they retain full control. Then there are the usual regular weekly current affairs programmes on both channels, which feature political parties and their policy plans at election times. Finally, and most important, are the special election programmes with nightly round-ups of the day's political speeches and events. The BBC's *Election Forum* and ITV's extended *News at Ten* have done much to explain politics to ordinary people. We know this from two major sociological studies made into aspects of the 1959, 1964 and 1966 elections.

The 1959 election, the first for four years, was studied in detail by the sociologists J. Trenaman and D. McQuail.[10] Their conclusion was that television merely increased voters' knowledge without altering their voting intentions. They failed to discover a correlation between television viewing and the changing of party affiliations, even when people changed the way in which they were going to vote during the campaign. In typically sociological language, they wrote of a 'barrier between sources of communication and movements of attitude in the political field at the General Election.' This remained the prevailing view for some time until Jay Blumler and Dennis McQuail published their *magnum opus* in 1968 entitled *Television in Politics – Its Uses and Influence*. Its title alone should have led us to expect to see the denizens of the Conservative

Central Office and of Transport House hurtling to the bookshops. But the truth was less dramatic than the title might lead us to expect.

Blumler's work was backed up by extensive questioning of those people who watched television most during the campaign. Why did they view? What programmes in particular had they watched? How had the television programmes that they watched affected them? The conclusions were that a large group of voters in 1964 were re-thinking their position right up to polling day, because of the passing of the Macmillan era of 'You've never had it so good'.

For 1964, television provided a vital source of fundamental impressions about party leaders, and a mine of information about the issues at stake. The old 'hypodermic' theory of cause and effect was replaced by a new sociological model that might be called the 'atmospheric' theory. The 1964 'atmosphere' was one of questioning; for the questioners television provided the answers as never before. Even the Labour slogan 'Thirteen Years Wasted' posed the question 'What was wasted?' and 'What should be done now?' Harold Wilson's 'white-hot technological revolution' line seemed to provide a modern argument and a modern atmosphere poles apart from the 'tweedy, belted earl' atmosphere of Sir Alec Douglas-Home's televised appearances. To quote just one example, Sir Alec's attempt to be folksy in admitting that he needed matchsticks to help him calculate aspects of the national budget provoked contemptuous reactions from many who felt that he was 'talking down' to them or, worse, that he was admitting to incompetence.

The 1964 election campaign brought into British politics many facets associated with American presidential politics. The concentration on the leader to the extent of assigning film-teams to cover him every moment of his nationwide tour, filming him eating, travelling, even sleeping and waking up, is an essentially transatlantic approach. Each night keynotes from the party leaders' speeches were compared and analysed exhaustively. Harold Wilson became particularly good at reserving a special nugget of his speech for the brief minute or two that he would be 'live' on transmission to the *Nine O'Clock News* audience.

In the 1966 election Edward Heath became adept at answering or challenging what Wilson had said earlier in the evening so that both the late news summary and the morning bulletins led with Heath's comment rather than Wilson's statement. By 1966 Wilson had become disenchanted with the BBC, though happy with the more respectful attitude shown by ITN. As a result the BBC's spectacular interview on board the victory train bringing the victorious Labour leader down from the north was abruptly cancelled, while ITN earned an exclusive interview with the triumphant Prime Minister. But this is to anticipate, for the seeds of Harold Wilson's television and electoral success were planted earlier on, before the election campaigns had started.

The Labour Party has traditionally elected its leaders. This custom is now followed by the Conservatives, ever since their retiring leader Harold Macmillan advised the Queen to send for Sir Alec Douglas-Home. His undemocratic act, though correct according to the prevailing Conservative orthodoxies of the day, saddled his party with a leader who, though possessing enormous personal charm, was possibly an electoral liability and certainly a television disaster. Harold Wilson, in contrast, had been elected leader of the Labour Party in February 1963, following the death of Hugh Gaitskell. His margin of victory over his rival George Brown had not been large – the voting was 144 to 103 votes of the Parliamentary Labour Party. From that day onward Harold Wilson determined to use press and television to provide him with maximum projection before the election, which might come later that year. In the event, Sir Alec held on till the last possible moment, which was the following October, thereby allowing his rival an extra twelve months in which to make his impact on the country through the media and in various other ways.

Mr Wilson's plan was simple. Faced by an 80 per cent

Conservative-controlled press, he had to maximize his impact through television, which was by statute compelled to give him at least equal time with his opponent, the resident Prime Minister. If anything he got more than 50 per cent of television's attention since, after thirteen years of Conservative rule, television was pining for a change. The fact that Wilson so obviously took television seriously flattered the producers.

In contrast, televising Sir Alec was a permanent headache for Conservative Central Office. Uncertain of his appearance on the screen and of his delivery, they were resistant to any plan to use him. There was also a standing BBC lighting instruction issued to all studio lighting directors, laying down a procedure so complicated that it took forty minutes of valuable studio rehearsal time while lighting and make-up staff struggled to give the unfortunate Prime Minister the appearance of a chin. Another lucky break made Harold Wilson's supremacy even more marked. His only rival, George Brown, made a fool of himself on ITV. Poor George had dined too well in Shoreditch when, unprepared, he was rushed to the ATV studio when news broke of President Kennedy's assassination.

From then on, up to the election, television tended to portray the party battle in largely personal terms – the 13th Earl of Home versus Mr Wilson, that likeable Yorkshireman with a friendly pipe. Wilson challenged Home to a series of television debates, as Kennedy had challenged Nixon. Wisely Sir Alec refused – and to most of us in television there was no doubt as to who would have won. I can well remember standing in the oak-panelled hospitality rooms of Lime Grove studios listening to Harold Wilson enthusing over White's book, *The Making of the President*, which he had recently read. His 'Kennedy-style' campaign was a triumphant success.

Great Britain: the television election
Until the 1959 General Election, television deliberately removed references to the election from news bulletins, and any programme that might have the faintest effect on the

balance of the parties was immediately cancelled. 1959 marked the beginning of television coverage of elections while the 1964 and 1966 elections marked the big breakthrough, with Harold Wilson the main benefactor. But Wilson emerged from the 1966 election with a deep sense of grievance against the BBC for what he regarded as his rough handling by them, and in the years that followed he appeared on television less and less frequently. After the 1967 devaluation he ceased giving any television interviews for nearly a year. By 1970 he was back on speaking terms with both broadcasting organizations and the first three general elections of the 1970's were to see the full emergence of the 'television election' pattern.

The marked difference between the old-style 'television coverage of the election' of the sixties and the 'television election' of the seventies is one of degree. In earlier days the election campaign was planned by the political parties without reference to the needs of television. Voters got to know about the issues from political meetings, poster-hoardings, the national press and local gossip. Today the shape of general election campaigns is moulded by the parties to suit the needs of television. The morning party press conferences are timed to suit television rather than the press, and are reported by television long before the press. Elaborate arrangements are made for camera positions and technical facilities; the dais is arranged like a studio set with massive colour-corrected lighting. The next appointment for the cameras will be at the carefully pre-arranged afternoon canvassing sessions, the so-called 'walkabout'. This provides visual material of leading party figures for the early evening news bulletins. In the evening, party leaders' set speeches are timed to provide extracts for the main BBC news or ITV's *News at Ten*. One neat, easily extractable chunk is provided in the speech for just this purpose.

Voters are exposed to ever more television about elections. The BBC devoted 33 per cent more time to the election in 1974 than in 1970. While newspapers *report* the campaign, television is actually the means whereby the election drama is unfolded. One leader makes a point on television one evening; as soon as he can manage it, often the same night, the other leader replies. Edward Heath became particularly adept at replying very late each night to a point made by Harold Wilson. This ensured that the morning bulletins would lead with his rejoinder, rather than Wilson's original point.

Just as Buckingham Palace makes careful arrangements with the television organizations before all-important royal occasions, so the parties influence what can and cannot be televised through the All-party Committee on Broadcasting, a serious misnomer for a group that until recently included only the Conservative, Labour and Liberal Parties (and which even now regards the emergence of new parties with the deepest misgivings). The parties are protected from the danger of editorializing by the BBC by the *Prescribing Memoranda*, and the 1954 Television Act imposes similar duties on Independent television. During an election campaign tremendous attention is paid to balance; every news bulletin will contain something about each party's 'walkabouts', news conferences and speeches, whether genuinely newsworthy or not. But this balance only applies to the big three parties; other groups are virtually ignored, though the nationalist groups in Scotland and Wales are getting increased regional coverage.

The type of programme format affects how politicians are portrayed. There are five main kinds: the interview, the inter-party discussion, the election forum, the news and the party political broadcast (very different in kind). The first four all include a television 'star' – the interview gives most scope to the star performer like Robin Day, because he both questions and responds. Even his tone can affect the character of the interview. But most important are the questions; does he ask the questions he thinks the audience wants answered, or the questions he thinks permissible without being accused of personal bias? My answer would be that interviewers ask what they consider permissible, and very often do not ask the full number of supplementaries that might be put in political debate, or by a member of the public in radio programmes like *Election Call*, where the questions have recently been notably blunt.

In contrast to the portrait of the interviewer as a member of the Inquisition grilling his victim, David Dimbleby has rightly pointed out that politicians try to fix the rules in their favour. 'Politicians have learnt a dozen ways of blunting the impact of television – expressing a preference for certain interviewers, being pernickety about their fellow interviewees, quibbling about the areas of questioning, and using diversionary tactics (if in doubt, attack the introduction of the item).'[11]

Interviewers have 'ground rules for the fair conduct of interviewing' according to the BBC's *Principles and Practice in News and Current Affairs*. Interviewers have an obligation to 'satisfy the enquiring mind of the public . . . while at the same time encouraging the person interviewed to display his case, or his thoughts, as he would wish'. In practice this means that 'private matters and the personal side of politics will receive little attention, and the interviewer is not expected to deal with the moral issues involved in particular policies. The interview will stay closely within the range of dissent and discussion covered by the two major parties. The interviewer will discuss the precise area of questioning in advance of the interview. The politician may veto the right of the interviewer to ask certain questions and the interviewer will respect that veto, because of his concern to ensure that the politician will be prepared to be interviewed on future occasions.'[12] This comment by John Dearlove is only part of the truth; some interviews are 'hard' and some are 'soft' only by accident. The third British Film Institute *Monograph* on television has reprinted two interviews by Robin Day, one a whimsical chat with Lord Hailsham, the other a rather more abrasive encounter with Edward Short. The fact that they were broadcast within a very short time of each other during the February 1974 election led to inevitable charges of bias.

The idea of the two or three parties discussing their differing policies in rational terms is very seldom realized in practice. What actually happens is that a politician has as much freedom to present his case as his opponents decide. The television 'star' plays the role of presenter/interviewer/chairman. But while his duty is sometimes seen as that of heaping coals on the fires of controversy, in fact the politicians have been known to gang up on him. They tend to arrange between themselves areas of disagreement or agreement, and defend these against the determination of the chairman to develop the discussion. I once invited Jo Grimond and Enoch Powell to debate defence on *Panorama*, confidently expecting a good discussion. But in fact they came to some arrangement in the hospitality suite, and the actual discussion was one of pretty uniform agreement with each other.

The Great Debate between party leaders has never yet happened, and probably never will; yet they regularly debate with each other in the House of Commons. Discussions between two politicians can be disappointing, but far more disappointing is the mass discussion with six or more taking part. Perhaps one of the best inter-party discussions took place during the February 1974 election between two retiring politicians, Sir John Foster (Conservative) and Richard Crossman (Labour). They included the meetings, party press conferences and meetings with voters and leaders with an easy confidence that made the television middlemen unnecessary. For once the viewer could really feel inside a mystery that he could witness but never share.

The All-party Committee on Political Broadcasting effectively bans live audiences and Sunday programmes for election broadcasting and insists on full consultation over both invitations to speakers and the choice of constituencies for survey. When in 1970 the BBC asked for two long debates on Sunday evenings, they were refused permission. Nor do the parties like the ideas of panels of questioners; they refuse to believe that television producers are capable of finding representative groups of questioners.

The All-party Committee acts as a restraint on broadcasters, but they have allowed election forum programmes since 1966. The idea is simple; viewers are asked to send in postcards with questions that can then be put to the politicians. The programme works well, though the exclusion of minor parties is regrettable. The Scottish Nationalists appealed to the courts because of their exclusion in 1970, but failed. Perhaps the best kind of election forum took place on radio, with the introduction of the phone-in in 1974. It provided marvellous broadcasting, but of the kind the parties would insist is restricted to radio.

The parties have least direct control over news broadcasts. These form the major vehicle of the television election in terms of time and audience. Television news introduces the real world into the area of election debate. In 1974 the February election was pregnant with real news that affected the parties. Affecting the Liberal Party was the news of the collapse of the London and Counties Securities Bank, of which Jeremy Thorpe was a director. Affecting the Labour Party was the news that Herr Scheel asserted there could be no renegotiation of Britain's entry to the EEC. After that came news that affected the Conservatives; first that there had been an error in calculating miners' pay; then the CBI General Secretary's declaration that he would scrap the Industrial Relations Act. Over-all the Conservatives suffered most.

Party political broadcasts began in 1951, and continue, though in disfavour with both the general public and television producers. Election party political broadcasts show the respective parties in curious lights; the Conservatives concentrate on expensive productions which are usually by far the most technically sophisticated. The Labour Party usually makes studio-based programmes, though occasionally uses filmed inserts. The Liberals, always short of money and air-time, concentrate on straight talks from their leaders.

Take for example the 1970 election. The Labour Party began the first of its five ten-minute programmes with a portrait of Harold Wilson at Downing Street, then followed with one showing Jim Callaghan at a Cardiff rally,

then a filmed programme on the social services; a fourth
programme had Roy Jenkins talking about the economy,
and a final programme showed Mr and Mrs Wilson. The
Liberals in contrast used Thorpe, followed by Grimond,
followed by Thorpe again. The Communists also used the
talk-to-camera approach for their single broadcast.

Conservative broadcasting preparations began over a
year before the election campaign. Using their two former
TV star performers, Chris Chataway and Geoffrey John-
son-Smith, they provided an election set which bore strong
resemblances to the *News at Ten* studio set, and their
broadcasts were actually transmitted at ten o'clock. Extensive and effective use was made of short film extracts of
street interviews of ordinary people. This 'vox pop'
material struck the 'hardest and lowest blows'.

Voice 6: 'My pay over the last twelve years has doubled,
but my standard of living has gone down by half.'

Voice 7: 'Oh, you take a pound note – it's gone. You
take a five pound note and that's gone. It's terrible.'

Voice 8: 'Bloody disgraceful.'

Voice 9: 'Terrible.'

Voice 10: 'Shocking.'

Voice 11: 'It's disgraceful. Everything's gone up. Tooth-
paste, baby clothes, baby food, everything you go for.'

Each of their four programmes began with the Chat-
away/Johnson-Smith dialogues which hit the government
with well-chosen, topical jibes. In the first programme,
following the 'vox pops', came a sympathetic Mr Heath
explaining that he understood why people felt let down. In
the second programme they used a wooden Lord Balneil
and a gentlemanly Reggie Maudling. In the third Mr Macleod said 'They (Labour) just don't care' and the final programme began with wedding bells and a housewife from
Wandsworth saying 'The Conservatives couldn't be worse
than Labour', and ended with a voice saying 'the wrong

decision could be expensive'. Mr Heath appeared for ten of the fifty minutes allowed to the Conservatives; Mr Wilson appeared for twenty of the fifty minutes allowed to Labour. But whether the polished Conservative Party political broadcasts were more effective than the Labour broadcasts is hard to say. BBC Audience Research and other evidence collected by the Conservatives is inconclusive. There were lovely summer evenings during the campaign and for those who chose to stay in and watch television, the World Cup matches were a bigger draw than the television election campaign.

In the February 1974 election there were again thirteen party political broadcasts shared in the same ratio of five Conservative and Labour to three Liberal ten-minute slots. The National Front qualified for five minutes by putting up fifty candidates, but the Communists did not and so lost their broadcast.

The Conservative broadcasts became more like advertising commercials than ever, which is hardly surprising considering they used the biggest film company specializing in TV commercials – James Garrett and Partners Limited. The first programme used 'vox pops' and a serious Mr Heath arguing the need to be firm but fair. The second programme used nurses and pensioners to support the government's record on social welfare and wages, which was defended by Sir Keith Joseph and William Whitelaw. But the programme ended with a 'commercial' showing a puppet Mr Wilson spitting out cash for miners, food subsidies and nationalization. The voice over said, 'Where does Harold Wilson get his money? From you . . .' The third Conservative broadcast produced an even bigger row, with a nationalization sequence that showed Labour taking over pay packets, bank accounts, mortgages and insurance policies. It ended with a young couple losing their house as the voice said, 'It wouldn't take much more of a move to the left and you could find yourself not even owning your own home.' Anthony Barber, clearly unaware of what had preceded him, then argued that democracy itself would be in danger if Labour won. University teacher and television expert Martin Harrison wrote a fitting epitaph on this abuse of screen freedom, 'This was a sorry broadcast in its ethical blindness, its clumsy cascade of visual gimmicks, and its abysmal view of the electorate's intelligence.'[13]

Labour's party politicals came under the operational control of their Broadcasting Officer, Doreen Stainforth, whose unmatched experience of what to do and what not to do extended over the previous decade. So though the Labour Party did commission three programmes from David Naden Associates, the 'adman' excesses were avoided. The general plan to promote the Labour 'team', put forward more specific policy plans and avoid bashing the Tories too much worked well. Jim Callaghan lamented the parlous state of the economy under the Tories, Shirley Williams showed 'then' and 'now' shopping-baskets, and Denis Healey lambasted the EEC bureaucrats. They had 'already instructed Mr Heath in the next two years to raise VAT by half and put VAT on food'. Though this was a minor inaccuracy compared with the Barber broadcast, few current affairs producers would have let such a remark be broadcast as a balanced statement about the EEC. Other programmes used Roy Jenkins to give the tone of civilized idealism, young candidates to talk of the future, and Harold Wilson for the final broadcast. This programme began with clips of eight future ministers who brought 'over forty years' experience as government ministers to the crisis', and ended with the leader offering Labour as the party which would restore fairness, direction, moderation and common sense.

The Liberal broadcasts were more adventurous than usual, thanks to the help of a retired BBC radio producer, Stephen Bonarjee. But the biggest sensation was produced by Plaid Cymru who successfully sued the BBC in the High Court over the BBC's attempt to alter the time of their broadcast. The BBC and IBA regional controllers had blithely allocated time for the two nationalist parties Plaid Cymru and the SNP on the final Tuesday before the election. The Conservatives then protested that this would 'spoil' Mr Heath's final appeal. All the members of the Committee on Broadcasting chimed in saying, correctly, that the last three broadcasts followed the pattern: Liberals, opposition, then government. Plaid Cymru demanded that the BBC should stick to the original time; the BBC replied that no other time except 17.05 on the Saturday preceding the election would be made available to them. Plaid Cymru's demand was supported by Mr Justice Bridge in the Queen's Bench Division of the High Court, and upheld on appeal. So Plaid Cymru got what they wanted, and after the election the so called All-party Committee on Broadcasting was enlarged to take in the Scottish Nationalists, but not Plaid Cymru.

With the referendum campaign all the usual political election-style programmes reappeared, though with mercifully less broadcasting time than during the 1974 elections. What was interesting was the prospect of party political broadcasts from two new groups BIE (Britain In Europe) and the opposite NRC (National Referendum Campaign). The former spent £105,000 on its broadcasts, the latter a mere £2,500. What cost the BIE so much was a trendy American film director who had worked for the Kennedy campaigns. But there was no comparable difference in the impact of the programmes. The four BIE presentations drew audiences of 22 million, the NRC presentations audiences of 20.6 million. The total audience for the referendum programmes was slightly above that for the two previous general elections. Anthony Smith of St Anthony's College, Oxford, wrote: 'Although the issues were complex and not novel, viewers and listeners proved unexpectedly willing to accept the great doses of exposition and debate which they received immediately before the day of decision. However, an elaborate study of public opinion conducted during and after the campaign jointly by the BBC and the ITA gave no support to those who argue that broadcasting tells people what to think.'[14]

One final point should be made about television coverage of election campaigns. There is an important quality of ritual that broadcasters bring to the occasion, a curious amalgam between the approach of commentators on the Grand National and those court reporters at a royal wedding. It is almost as though Ladbrokes were taking bets on a race that began at the pithead or country estate, but led via the Television Centre to Downing Street.

Priests of this event are easily recognizable as they are brought out of seclusion for the great election results programme. Dr David Butler is really the historian/pope of the evening; his books on the event flow as inevitably as the Thames flows past Westminster. Professor Robert MacKenzie is the Merlin-figure – impishly producing amazing and unlikely results from his swingometer with all the gravity of a liberated academic. For ITV Professor Richard Rose provides a special blend of knowledge about the greatest political race of the decade, or so he would have us believe.

Trevor Pateman describes the Television Election as an event 'which accords special treatment to all the participants, politicians and voters alike: the politicians are foregrounded, their authority reinforced; the voters are reassured of their importance to the democratic process.'[15] And from the moment that Wagner's *Ride of the Valkyries* heralds the opening credits of the election results programme, we know that a very special ritual is to be unfolded to us, brought to us, the great watching congregation, by our television political-priesthood. Governments may rise or fall, but the Robin Days of our screen are always with us, unfolding the mystery of politics through the long hours of the night until the dawn breaks, and a new Prime Minister can make his way to the Palace.

Should we televise Parliament?

For all the talk of open government, the Houses of Parliament remain a secret place. During the eighteenth century members of Parliament fought a long battle against journalists' demands for the right to report debates. The late twentieth century has seen the same struggle over the right to broadcast proceedings. Even after the Second World War MPs on both sides were totally opposed to the idea. A very cautious beginning was made in 1959 with the televising of the state opening of Parliament by the Queen. Supporters of the moves to televise the normal proceedings of the Commons hailed this as a break-through. Robin Day wrote that 'it enabled all the people to witness an ancient parliamentary ritual previously seen only by a privileged few. As a television spectacle it was second only in splendour to the Coronation'. The following year Nye Bevan advocated 'a serious investigation into the technical possibilities of televising Parliamentary proceedings'. As a result of this the government asked the BBC to make a report, but nothing came of it.

In 1963 a full-scale Commons debate took place on parliamentary reform, and the idea of televising Parliament came in for some scathing criticism by the Labour Chief Whip Mr Herbert Bowden (later Lord Aylestone, Chairman of the IBA). 'I do not like the idea . . . I do not want Parliament to become an alternative to *That Was The Week That Was*, *Steptoe and Son* or *Coronation Street*.' But other influential voices, including the future Prime Minister James Callaghan, were in favour, and Iain MacLeod, Leader of the House, proclaimed his support.

Five years passed, and in 1968 a cautious closed-circuit experiment was carried out by the House of Lords. The next cautious step came in 1975 with a massive vote in favour of the radio broadcasting of Parliament. An experiment was a great success, and now in 1976 there are plans for regular live coverage of the House by both BBC and commercial radio, together with edited programmes late at night. But the doors remain firmly shut to cameras.

The arguments for televising Parliament are strong. First it would mean that authentic political debates could be seen – which would be far preferable to the mock-encounters so often seen on our screens. Parliament would benefit from this exposure. Second, no longer would the decision as to which MPs are permitted to appear be the monopoly of television producers whose political judgement has sometimes been known to err. Thirdly, the Opposition would benefit considerably; at present the party in power benefits most from television coverage, since what government Ministers do is essentially more newsworthy than what the shadow Ministers do. Some of the problems of artificiality in political television would be solved too: 'Ministerial' broadcasts would be less necessary, and party political broadcasts might die out altogether.

Robin Day, always the leading advocate of televising Parliament, and from whom many of the ideas in this section were culled, sees a more glorious future for a televised Commons. He believes it would stimulate the House to modernize its procedure and improve the standard of debate, and that television offers a 'measureless opportunity for rekindling interest in Parliament'. Others are more guarded, but if, as confidently expected, the radio broadcasts are a success, then surely television cameras should follow where the microphone has led. And though the plans have always been only for edited versions of debates to be transmitted, the existence of a fourth and even fifth channel after the report of the Annan Committee might make all-day live coverage possible. But would there be an audience for continuous Commons debates?

Chapter Seven

Television and Belief – the Thomas Syndrome

'Unless I see the mark of the nails on his hands, unless I put my finger into the place where the nails were, and my hand into his side, I will not believe it.' *Thomas, in John's Gospel*

'Religion like politics calls for a choice and for commitment, an informed choice, or acceptance based on ignorance and inertia.' So wrote John Scupham, a former head of BBC Educational Broadcasting. To read this chapter, or to skip it and go on to the next, demands a choice which may well be based on personal conviction. So I should declare my personal position at the outset. I subscribe to a committed Christian position, but do not watch religious television often. I have never held the view that belief and commitment must be compartmentalized or reserved for Sundays. For Christians and agnostics alike it is relevant to ask whether current religious television is satisfactory, and, at a deeper level, whether religious television as such is really necessary.

To begin with, a brief glance at the religious profile of Britain in the third quarter of the twentieth century, to see how fast attitudes are changing. In 1960 a survey carried out by the Gallup Poll organization for ABC Television Ltd sampled their adult viewing population in London, the Midlands and the North. The results were surprising. Nearly all those questioned regarded themselves as belonging to a religious denomination. Sixty-seven per cent classified themselves as belonging to the Church of England. Four in every five interviewed believed in some kind of God – only two per cent were convinced atheists. Twenty-five per cent of the sample said they went to a place of worship once a month. (Were they telling the truth?)

Ten years later the 1970 ITA Survey showed that religious broadcasting reaches two-thirds of the population. Fifty-six per cent of viewers claim to pay attention to religious broadcasting, while a further 24 per cent 'leave the set on but don't really listen'. A third of the self-styled 'strongly religious' and one half of the 'not very religious' claim that they deliberately switch on to watch a religious programme. The ITV programme *Stars on Sunday* produced by Yorkshire Television got a regular audience of twelve to fifteen million. The composition of that audience is similar to that for *Coronation Street*.

Religious broadcasting holds a privileged position within both television channels. Until recently both sides have preserved a 'protected hour' between 6.15 p.m. and 7.20 p.m. on Sundays. The BBC Religious Broadcasting Department provides between two and three hours a week of religious television, and nine hours of religious radio on Radios 2 and 4. At the time of writing ITV provides two to three hours of religious programmes every Sunday plus late-night weekday programmes as well. The BBC probably spends about two million pounds a year on religious programmes, the ITV companies an estimated half of that amount, but they publish no figures of expenditure.

The BBC defines the aims of its religious broadcasting very clearly: 'The first aim is that it should reflect the worship, thought and action of those Churches which represent the mainstream of the Christian tradition in the country. The second is that religious broadcasting should bring before listeners and viewers what is most significant in the relationship between the Christian faith and the modern world. The third aim is that religious broadcasting should seek to reach those on the fringe of the organized life of the Churches or quite outside it.'

The BBC clearly aims at three different audiences, namely:

    a. the great majority of viewers and listeners who are not members of a congregation.

    b. a minority of actively committed church-going Christians who view and listen.

    c. committed Christians prevented by illness or age from taking an active part in a church.

Much of the dissatisfaction with religious programming expressed by church members arises because they fail to realize that different audiences demand different programme approaches. Before it is possible to discuss programmes for group a intelligently it is necessary to make four sub-divisions, dependent on programme aims and types. Group a1 programmes could be categorized as directly evangelistic, aiming 'to bring men and women to (deeper) commitment to Christ in the Fellowship of His Church'.[1] Group a2 from the general audience might turn off programmes which are avowedly evangelistic, but are quite content to watch or to listen to programmes which portray 'realities beyond the material and sensuous'. Such programmes would include *Stars on Sunday* and *Songs that Matter*. Group a3 are those in the general audience who enjoy the 'sacred concert' approach of *Songs of Praise* and similar programmes. Group a4 are those in the general audience prepared to listen to panel discussions and interviews which relate the Christian faith to the daily realities of life.

BBC and ITV religious output

Meeting Point, A Chance to Meet, The Question Why and *The Sunday Debate* all cater for the general, non-committed viewer in category a4. These programmes have often been produced by displaced current affairs directors transferred to Religious Broadcasting while BBC staff administration wonder what next to do with them. Often the programmes have presented eminent and interesting men who have rarely been able, in the limited time, to present adequately 'the reason for the hope that is in them'. The compères vary from Robin Day playing the role of an agnostic umpire to Malcolm Muggeridge playing the role of God's umpire on a bad wicket in failing light. Too often the programmes get interesting in the last three minutes – overfilling the studio with 'representative opinion' is one reason for this.

The second type of Sunday offering is usually a hymn-singing programme such as *Songs of Praise*, *Sing a New Song* or *The Choice is Yours*. Rows of singers, stained glass and gothic arches emphasize that the church retains its Victorian middle-class orientation. The religious message is not clear enough to make anyone feel uncomfortable, and the viewing figures are good. Televised church services are well produced but, unless the church happens to have a fiery preacher, the comfortable, complacent feelings engendered by the 'sacred concert' approach are evoked again by the broadcast services. No doubt the services are much appreciated by the housebound, though I am not aware of any audience research among the housebound and hospitalized to bear out these impressions.

Some of the most interesting BBC programmes are the late-evening *Viewpoint* series, which profile interesting Christians, and the occasional prestige documentaries. Of the latter, *Padre Pio* and *Something Beautiful for God* (a portrait of Mother Theresa of Calcutta) were outstanding. Such documentaries are rare because of the cost. Similar programmes are sometimes produced by missionary societies, but can never hope for BBC transmission. Its *amour propre* does not allow it. The excuse usually offered is that the missionary films are not good enough. That this is not always true will be borne out by any who have seen the Missions to Seamen film *I Was A Stranger*, and the Church Missionary Society film *Mission Incomplete*.

The ITV religious output comes mostly from the five major network companies, LWT, Thames, ATV, Granada and Yorkshire. Of the 104 ITV religious slots available each year the big four take 85 to 90, and the little regional companies between ten and fifteen. Yet, surprisingly, the regional companies produce some of the best. Tyne-Tees Television produced a marvellous six-programme series with Cliff Richard, retelling Gospel parables in modern form. Though described in the *ITV Yearbook* as 'perhaps ITV's most notable attempt . . . to use the resources and panache of television for an evangelistic message' the series was never shown nationally. Network jealousies are powerful. One may speculate that the big five were not going to allow a small regional company to muscle in on their share of the programme slots.

The 'big five' have not excelled themselves in this field since the new licences were awarded in 1968. ATV's *Beyond Belief* was a brave attempt to be funny, which failed. Granada's *Seven Days* was a good current affairs programme, but not able to contribute much in terms of Christian insights. London Weekend's *Roundhouse* failed for most people, and their long series on people who had left the church was produced by a delightful ex-Roman Catholic priest who was busy rethinking his own position. This the programmes all too clearly illustrated.

Of the ITV religious programming successes, *Adam Smith* – a drama series from Granada – and *Stars on Sunday* – the sentimentalized fantasy world of Yorkshire's religious light entertainment spectacular – are by far the most interesting. *Adam Smith* was as good as most drama series of its kind can be. The television critic Monica Furlong asked how, apart from the calling of its hero, the series differed from one that might be sponsored by the British Humanist Association. *Stars on Sunday* is specifically Christian in what some would regard as the most cloying way. Does the Christian content survive the chocolate-box presentation? Many would argue that it does, not least the Yorkshire Television religious adviser, the Rev. Brandon Jackson, who himself wrote some of the scripts.

Outside the religious slots both channels treat Christianity in a questioning vein. John Gow's *Panorama* portrait, *The Church of England Today*, described as a 'caricature' by the Church Information Office was the predictable hatchet job that *Panorama* producers excel at. Present the old and reactionary versus the young and progressive (even if the chief progressive spokesman, Nicholas

Stacey, has left the Church of England) and you can't go wrong. Despite public and private protests, the BBC was unrepentant. Every current affairs producer knows that to slander an institution is safe enough; slandering individuals can involve apologies.

However, current affairs programmes are not always hostile to the Christian point of view. While the radio programme *The World This Weekend* attacked the 1971 *Festival of Light* in what the Church Information Office regarded as a biassed report, *Midweek* on BBC 1 did an admirably objective report on the Northern *Festival of Light*. Sensible churchmen should not object to even-handed reporting; and of course there were aspects of both Festivals that could be criticized.

It is the duty of the programme editors to ensure that justice is done to Christian matters by representing both favourable and unfavourable verdicts. Unfortunately, while in political matters impartiality is nearly always preserved, because of the army of party officials on both the Conservative and Labour sides determined to see that justice is done, in Christian matters the churches carry much less weight and distortion easily creeps in.

The treatment of Christianity in drama and light entertainment programmes varies enormously. The *Report* of the Broadcasting Commission of the General Synod of the Church of England provided a useful description of what a Christian approach to drama might imply: 'The Christian faith is trinitarian and incarnational. The image of the Trinity affirms that the power behind all phenomena is a power of relationship – mutual, self-limiting and self-offering. In the Incarnation Christians see that relationship in human form in the person of Jesus Christ. It follows, therefore, that Christian society must endeavour to conform to the pattern of Christ. Drama, then, can be called Christian if it explores with integrity and compassion the expression of the faith, in all human relationships whether Godward or manward, and whether the work treats of failure or success. A valid complaint against much television drama is that it is shallow in conception and shows man as sub-human, self-enclosed and without hope.'

In that much modern drama shows man as being without hope, because it portrays the philosophical despair of many serious dramatists today, much television drama could not possibly be called Christian. For the church the long-term answer to this problem is to encourage Christian playwrights. Writers like John Antrobus, Murray Watts and Leo Aylen deserve much greater support from Christians than they actually receive. In the last five years both the Arts Centre Group and the Fellowship of Christians in the Arts have made big efforts to encourage Christians in all spheres of the arts, and new Christian writers in particular. But this positive work receives much less notice in the Christian press than the endless pronouncements of viewers like Mrs Whitehouse, who were shocked by some item.

As the criteria of the NVALA are by no means philosophically definable, nor specifically Christian, it is not surprising to find a certain impatience with their pronouncements among creative people. The shock waves generated in Christian circles by a sincere and moving play by Dennis Potter entitled *Son of Man* at least produced some worthwhile debate. Following his attack on the Labour party in *Vote, Vote for Nigel Barton*, Potter endeavoured to strip away the coverings of the Gospel story and interpret it in humanist terms. One critic wrote that 'it is hard to believe that the BBC would have presented a play about Mahommed or Gandhi which was as unjust to them as *Son of Man* was to Jesus of Nazareth'. The Bishop of Bristol speaking in the Church Assembly was both more generous and more perceptive. He said that 'although many criticisms were voiced of the play – the thing that stood out most clearly was that the young author, facing the realities of his personal situation with courage, had a vision of the character of Jesus, and a conscience as a dramatist, which made it his own highest social responsibility to present what Jesus was in terms of effective drama'.

Comedy and light entertainment have long found legitimate targets in monks and clergymen, though the endless repetition of stereotypes can be criticized as being without insight or aim. Take for example the Vicar in *Dad's Army* who survives as timelessly as Mr Chadband in Charles Dickens' *Bleak House*. Many Christians find the dialogue passages in *Till Death Us Do Part* blasphemous; Alf's defence of the church and the monarchy made many Christians uncomfortable. The episode 'God. Mary and the Pill' brought apologies from the then Chairman of the BBC, Lord Hill.

Religious radio programmes

Though this book is primarily about British television, a balanced picture of the religious programmes available must include some reference to radio. Many feel radio to be a much better medium for Christian broadcasting. Vernon Sproxton, for long a key figure in the BBC Television Religious Department remarked: 'There are peculiar difficulties about transmitting grace . . . it tends to disappear as the cameras move in.' It is often argued that radio does better and cheaper what television fails to achieve because of the difficulties of visualizing. By its very nature it calls for a more imaginative response. Guthrie Moir, former Head of Religious and Educational Programmes at Thames TV, perceptively remarked that the churches have a 'verbal rather than visual gospel, sometimes better passed on by radio than by television'.

The BBC Network output of religious radio programmes exceeds thirty a week, apart from a wide variety of offerings on local radio. Commercial radio provides further opportunities. Capital Radio and London Broadcasting have achieved some lively programmes, particularly in religious phone-ins. Most of the BBC output is non-controversial. The four series of daily programmes, *Prayer for the Day*, *Thought for the Day*, *Pause for Thought* and the *Daily Service*, the Saturday programmes *Outlook* and *Lighten our Darkness*, and the mass of services, discussions, hymn-singing and magazine programmes provide an outlet for a wide variety of tastes.

Religious education broadcasting provides still more airtime for Christians, with general interest items, morning prayers with interesting stories for younger children, and analytical programmes on contemporary religion for senior forms. Though the Broadcasting Commission of the Church of England did suggest that there should be programmes for Sunday schools, clergy and religious education teachers as well, it seems unlikely that the audience for still more religious programmes would be large enough to make the expense of broadcasting justifiable.

Certain articulate Christian pressure groups would clearly like to see a return to Reithian days, when devotional talks were commonplace and the microphone seemed to have been trapped in the chancel for long periods on Sundays. This school of thought comes very close to trying to hand over to the broadcasters the evangelistic and teaching tasks which are more properly the day-to-day responsibility of the churches themselves. The implication behind much discussion at Christian conferences is that if only the BBC was more helpful, somehow Britain would be a more Christian country.

It is only necessary to consider the elaborate consultative machinery established between the churches and the broadcasters to understand the myopia of such comments. The Central Religious Advisory Committee (CRAC) is an interdenominational group dating from the early days of the BBC, but performing the same advisory role for the ITV companies, who also have their own religious advisers. Traditionally chaired by an Anglican bishop, it is a pillar of orthodox views. As with educational broadcasting, the BBC and the commercial companies have no pet doctrinal views of their own; it would be deplorable if they did.

The task of broadcasting religious programmes is directly comparable with broadcasting political and sociological programmes, admirably summed up by Sir Hugh Greene: 'The main purpose of broadcasting, I suggest, is to make the microphone and the television screen available to the widest possible range of subjects, and to the best exponents available of the differing views on any given subject, to let the debate decide or not as the case may be, and in Cardinal Heenan's words "to merge with a deeper knowledge".[2]

Should broadcasting be evangelistic?

Evangelism is a broad term and it has been broadly interpreted. As long ago as 1948 the Central Religious Advisory Committee insisted that religious broadcasting should 'reflect and proclaim the faith of the Church as it is actually found in the Bible, and in the living traditions and liturgical life and preaching of the visible Christian churches'. To that majority of viewers and listeners who may be uninitiated, or sceptical, or both, these 'living traditions and liturgical life' can often seem irrelevant and out of date. How far away from the reality is the image of the church projected by broadcasters?

In 1963 a Christian group at William Temple College, Rugby, compared all religious programmes in a given month with the services of twenty-three churches of all denominations in the area. They found that the broadcasts fairly represented the average level of 'the worship, thought and action of those churches which represent the main stream of the Christian tradition in the country'. This average level they deemed to be not nearly good enough. The church, they felt, seemed to be 'inward-turned, pre-occupied with its own role in the world, yet imperfectly aware of what was going on there'. Its hymns, like its homilies, were often more comforting than challenging; its theology untroubled by the findings of scholarship, or the crises of new thought; its estimate of human nature low; and its attitude to the outside world pessimistic, timid and remote. Contact with reality was only established in programmes like *Meeting Point* and *Sunday Break*. There, at least, felt the report, 'there is an acknowledgment that not all the worthwhile people in the world are Christians. There is an honest attempt to face up to contemporary problems, and to present differing points of view about them.'

This survey embraced both radio and television. What defence can we give to the criticisms made? One could argue that it is natural to find the church concerned about its own role in the world. If its hymns, like its homilies, are more comforting than challenging, perhaps that is what many listeners expect of broadcast religion. If the sermons which are broadcast are 'untroubled by the findings of scholarship or the crises of new thought', that does not mean that religious broadcasting has everywhere ignored the writings of Dr Robinson, Dietrich Bonhoeffer and Karl Barth (indeed some would say that it has paid undue attention to the new theology). If the church's 'estimate of human nature is low', it can be argued that the church is being true to man's condition as portrayed in the Bible, and to the doctrine of original sin. If 'the church's attitude to the outside world is pessimistic, timid and remote', the reply to this charge could be that it is good to hear men and women who reject the facile optimism of the woolly humanist, the advertiser and the disc jockey who tell us glibly that all is for the best in this best of all possible worlds.

Lord Ramsey, former Archbishop of Canterbury, once told Kenneth Harris that in his view religious television should help the committed Christian to 'an intelligent and thoughtful commitment instead of an unintelligent one, a commitment that has more thought of obligation to all those outside'. He felt that for the mildly interested viewer there should be 'programmes that challenge him to decision and help him to make his own faith and decision articulate'.

Programmes like *Meeting Point* and *The Sunday Debate* have made a serious attempt to examine the social implications of the gospel, and have done it well. To show that Christians care and do something about homelessness, for example, may be as effective a method of using television for evangelism as the direct appeal for commitment. To see Christians in action, to hear their achievements talked about, and to discern some of the depth of meaning to them of the gospel's message, challenge the casual viewer's idea of the Christian and the faith which motivates him.

The religious programme is not a comparable alternative to the evangelistic sermon. The traditional role of the sermon has been to instruct, to delight and to influence the will. Religious television programmes are very different from sermons in structure and content: they sometimes delight, but seldom instruct, because the vast majority of the television audience is very unwilling to be instructed. Can they influence the will? The impact of television is fundamentally different from the impact of the preacher in person delivering a challenge to decision for Christ. Any challenge presupposes a 'person-to-person' communication situation. Television is not 'person-to-person' even when one viewer sits alone absorbed by what is happening on the screen. Feedback is impossible. There is no chance to say, 'Stop. I don't understand.'

Some Christians will point to the evangelistic success of the closed-circuit broadcasts made by Billy Graham on his last campaign in Britain. But those broadcasts are not directly comparable with an evangelistic appeal on the television screen. Instead of sitting by their firesides at home, the audience had gone to special halls for an event, and if moved by what the evangelist said, they were immediately drawn into conversation by teams of experienced 'counsellors', who could respond to questions and expand on points made by the preacher. The viewer at home has no chance to use his will, to take up the challenge of decision.

A fairer description of the role of religious television would be 'pre-evangelistic'. The last two decades have seen the rise of increasing resistance to indoctrination of any kind. The success of television advertising persuasion techniques is undeniable, but at the same time there is a healthy scepticism about big claims. *Ex cathedra* statements are treated with reserve, especially by young people. For the young audience exposition must be open-minded and open-ended if it is to succeed. Today's generation of young truth-seekers may be sceptical, and often ignorant of the claims and the biblical sources of Christianity, but they are also often receptive to ideas which are new to them. Many of the *Meeting Point* and *Sunday Debate* programmes are aimed at this audience. Such programmes do not always please the orthodox, but are probably the more effective because they do break away from the orthodox framework of nineteenth-century evangelistic sermons, eighteenth-century hymns and seventeenth-century liturgy. However, proof that these programmes are successful in their own terms is hard to come by; little audience research has yet been done, although the IBA Religious Advisory section has done some pioneering work in this area.

During the later sixties the BBC under Sir Hugh Greene reacted to the changing theological climate by giving an uncritical welcome to what conservative Christian thinking regarded as dangerously liberal theologians. Dr Robinson and his supporters talked about God as the 'ground of our being' so often that the satirist Alan Bennett of *Beyond the Fringe* fame took to parodying the words. Religious television began to embrace a wide range of subjects. Penry Jones, a man of wide experience who had controlled religious programmes first on ITV then on BBC, went on record as saying that 'all television is religious television'. More and more religious programmes began to look at current affairs, and the difference between religious current affairs and the normal current affairs output became marginal. In 1972 the IBA actually had to forbid London Weekend Television broadcasting a series of interview programmes within the Sunday 18.15 'closed period' on the grounds that, according to press reports 'the interviews did not touch upon religion'.

Religious producers began to state categorically that persuasion was not the purpose of their programmes. One BBC religious producer said, 'My aim is not to persuade, but to attract and present.' A colleague added, 'nor is persuasion possible'. Advocates of hard- and soft-line religious broadcasting began leaping to their feet at such gatherings as the Church of England's Church Assembly debate on broadcasting in 1970. Some speakers claimed that religious programmes showed 'a tragic lack of Christian content', others that 'there is too great a predominance of the discussion and debate element over proclamation and teaching'. Others complained that participants were 'donnish' and that excessive opportunities were given to 'liberals, agnostics and atheists'. One attacker said that there was a 'complete absence of any kind of evangelical voice among clergy who have appeared'. The Church Information Office, an Anglican body, alleged that there was 'what appears to be an emaciated and tentative faith in which the Christian certainties are never adequately expressed'.

None summed up the whole situation in a more masterly way than the Rev. Michael Saward, former Anglican Radio and Television Officer, when he described three possible approaches to what religious broadcasting is all about:

1 *Religion equals life.* The sacred and the secular are regarded as being co-extensive and co-terminous. According to this view every programme is religious if it 'evokes a religious response'.

2 *Religion is the relationship between God and the individual soul.* The sacred and secular are set in opposition to each other. This view sees broadcast religion primarily in terms of direct evangelism.

3 *Religion is the relationship between God and the soul worked out in every aspect of life.* The sacred and the secular are related but not co-terminous. This view seeks to bring the supernatural to bear upon the whole range of human concern.

Attitudes at the Church Assembly debate in 1970 tended to polarize between those who adopted the so-called 'softline' and agree broadly with the attitudes contained in the first approach above and the 'hard-liners' who agreed with the second approach. The latter were alleged to be interested only in direct evangelistic proclamation on television, while the former liked to project themselves as eminently reasonable men who had wide sympathies but who sincerely believed that explicit proclamation of the gospel was inappropriate in television programmes. They believed that the Christian truths are revealed incognito rather than by advertisement.

The third approach appears to be the most constructive. The former Archbishop of Canterbury, Lord Ramsey, should have the final word. In a speech to an ITA Religious Consultation he urged that religious television should 'depict human problems as they are, human situations just as they are, arouse interest in them as human situations and then see what the Christian faith can do with those situations in a practical way, not only by giving an ethical answer, but also by bringing something supernatural on to the human scene that alters the whole human perspective and enables the whole human problem to be tackled'.

Do we sincerely want religious television?

All in all, do we the viewers sincerely want religious television? What does it add, within its privileged hour, or late at night, which would stand up in the competitive atmosphere of normal programme scheduling? Programme planners would probably largely consent to our continued reception of televised services, and to the inclusion of discussion programmes on matters which affect the Christian conscience as part of public affairs. Archbishops should get their share of interviewing by Robin Day and David Frost along with politicians and show-business personalities. The programme planners might even agree that the peak-viewing 6.15 p.m. spot on Sunday nights might remain. Other religious programmes might also get a showing, although many would simply disappear, a not-undeserved fate. But we, the viewers, must question whether God needs this special treatment at the hands of programme planners when the churches are losing ground. More people are going to be convinced, challenged and changed by face-to-face encounters with real Christians than by watching God-preaching through the tube.

Who wants Christian television programmes? Not agnostics, atheists, Buddhists, Muslims and the great body of 'don't knows'. Not even, perhaps, the ever-dwindling bands of churchgoers, who do not watch it themselves but criticize it so often that they can hardly insist that others should watch.

Who wants Christian television programmes? Viewers, whether or not committed to any particular faith, should welcome any programme which aims to illuminate. Unfortunately Christian ghetto broadcasting (that is, programmes addressed exclusively to the adherents of the stricter forms of Christianity) is continually being demanded by certain pressure groups, and the recent submissions to the Annan Committee show that their requests continue. The programmes they ask for would be incomprehensible to those who do not know the language of their sub-culture.

Radio is much the better medium for dealing with those requests from the small minorities. Christian radio broadcasting has enjoyed a distinguished reputation for more than fifty years. Devotional, instructional and occasionally evangelistic religious broadcasting has catered well for those who wish to hear that sort of programme. Those against religious broadcasting argue that the place of religious radio is a privileged one, undeserved in terms of listening figures, or the percentage of citizens who have anything to do with Christianity.

However the humanist argument against religious programmes ignores the fact that it is the business of both radio and television to cater for the needs of minorities. Among minorities, the religious minority is a large one. James Gordon, Managing Director of Radio Clyde, Glasgow, made this point forcefully when he said in a Radio 3 programme, 'We decided to have religious broadcasting on Radio Clyde, simply because religion plays such a large part in the lives of the community we aim to serve. Twenty-five to thirty per cent of the population in our coverage area are at church on a Sunday. That means that going to church is the largest single out-of-home leisure activity in our area, short of dropping in on the pub or visiting friends. There are more people at church on a Sunday than there are at a football match, even in football-mad Glasgow on a Saturday afternoon. No one suggests we should not cover sport on a Saturday afternoon. I think it is equally obvious that we should be covering religion.'[3]

The BBC policy of responding to the audience's need echoes the point made by James Gordon for commercial radio. Speaking in a personal capacity as a practising Roman Catholic, rather than as Director-General of the BBC, Charles Curran said, 'I suppose some people would like to see it [religious broadcasting] as a kind of evangelical mission to the country, a sort of missionary call in the BBC to convert the whole country back, as people would say, to Christian belief and Christian practice. Now, I don't think that, as a practical matter, we can say that. What we are doing, in my view, is responding to a need in the audience, as we respond to other needs, and the need is represented by that group of practising and believing Christians who expect to see reflected in their broadcasting system a response to their belief and their commitment, just as other groups expect to see similar responses in other fields.'[4]

For many Sir Charles Curran has summed up the present position admirably. Once upon a time the BBC had an evangelistic purpose; the *BBC Handbook* for 1928 actually stated that 'The BBC is doing its best to prevent any decay of Christianity in a nominally Christian country'. Now it no longer does this. 'The broad aims of religious broadcasting are to present the worship, thought and action of the churches, to explore the contemporary relevance of the Christian faith for listeners and viewers, whether church members or not, and to reflect fresh religious insights.'

So the eighty-strong members of the BBC Religious Department and a similar number in ITV and commercial radio spread their energies over a wide range of Christian broadcasting. They provide worship, ecclesiastical news and views, a forum for contemporary religion, a debating chamber for the debate between Christianity and Humanism, even a reflection of the British way of life at the level of State religious observance in ceremonies like the coronation. They even broadcast evangelistic services occasionally. Between the entrenched positions of the various denominations, they tread a delicate path. It is more peaceful not to give offence; it could even be regarded as a more Christian way of broadcasting. All in all, we probably get the Christian broadcasting we deserve; perhaps we get better Christian broadcasting than we realize.

Chapter Eight

Sociology and Mass Media

In the Middle Ages, as now, man required entertainment, information and 'orientation'—long before printed books, newspapers, film and television were invented. Entertainment was provided for him by stories, often told by parents to children. The 'entertainment industry' consisted of ballad singers, minstrels and groups of actors, for whom folk tales, fairy tales and morality stories provided a reasonably wide range of basic material. In addition, the pageantry of church and State, part ritual, part entertainment, provided spectacles for the past as it does today.

Communications in past times

Information and news travelled by word of mouth. Communication took place where it does today – in markets, inns and private houses. Since people's lives in medieval times were largely directed by custom, in which superstition and irrationality played its part, custom modified the content of what was communicated to them. 'Feedback' was good, because communication was almost entirely 'face-to-face', and could be modified to suit the emotional and behavioural reaction of the audience. The communicator's success depended on his skill and personality. If he failed to get his message across, he soon knew of his failure.

'Orientation' could be described as the effects of culture, custom and religious teaching and traditions, which helped medieval man to steer himself through the age to which he belonged. Much orientation was implicit rather than explicit.

The next phase of communications history embraces the period from the late fifteenth to the middle of the nineteenth century. Protestantism emerged as a powerful new force, its progress matched by the growth of new nation-states, and big changes in commercial and economic life. Although the old forces of church and nobility, tradition and status were still important, the Protestant business-man, be he farmer or merchant, was increasingly indepen-dent in attitude and conscience. Because he could read his Bible, he could orientate himself through his reading of Scripture as well as through his conversation and observa-tions.

Entertainment was provided by the same means as in the Middle Ages, although there were important develop-ments in the theatre before Cromwell's Commonwealth put a temporary stop to such frivolities. The number of presses grew to match the rise of literacy levels, and books and newssheets became more common. However, there was one loss; direct feedback. Publishers and printers now came between the communicator and his audience. Fortu-nately what was lost in direct communication was more than made up for by the outlets provided for new talent. Printers and publishers constantly sought new authors to cater for the ever-growing circle of literate people anxious for reading matter.

This continued until finally, by the end of the nine-teenth century, the rapid growth of both mass production and mass literacy had completely altered the patterns and relationships of communications. A huge new public could afford to buy cheap, disposable newspapers and magazines – at the same shops where they bought a whole host of other consumer products. Communication became mass com-munication; society became mass society. Villagers and townsmen became interested in the daily events of an ever-widening world.

'Other-directed' attitudes

Among the many effects of the rise of mass society was the growth of a new attitude which increasingly affected the printed word, and later the new electronic media. This new attitude can be described loosely as 'deference to the presumed value standards of others'. The essence of much advertising and salesmanship is to inculcate what sociologists refer to as 'other-directed' attitudes. We might loosely describe this partly as the pressure to 'keep up with the Joneses'. To use a different analogy, it might be said that the gyroscope of the individual conscience which provided the 'orientation' for seventeenth-century man became increasingly superseded by the radar of the 'other-directed' twentieth-century man. This twentieth-century person guides himself according to the standards of his peer group as presented by the media. Spurred on by the needs of advertisers, from whom most of the agencies of mass communication derive their revenues, the agencies create and spread new norms. So contemporary group loyalties matter more than individual conscience and tradition.

In a bitter attack, the American sociologist C. Wright Mills wrote: 'Without common values and mutual trust, the cash nexus that links one man to another in transient contact has been made subtle in a dozen ways, and made to bite deeper into all areas of life and relations. People are required by the salesman ethic and convention to pretend interest in others in order to manipulate them. In course of time and as this ethic spreads it is gotten onto. Still it is conformed to as part of one's job and one's life style, but now with a winking eye, for one knows that manipulation is inherent in every human contact. Men are estranged from one another as each secretly tries to make an instrument of the other, and in time a full circle is made; one makes an instrument of himself, and is estranged from it also.'[1]

This is a tragic picture of twentieth-century man, corrupted by a sales-orientated society. Its message 'Buy, buy, buy!' is both implicit and explicit in all mass media. It is seen at its most blatant in American radio and television. There the advertiser himself sponsors the programme, and hence can dictate content, eliminating all references to facts which could reflect unfavourably on his product. What oil company would sponsor a programme about the pollution caused by motor vehicle exhausts?

Loss of feedback

The twentieth century has seen the final diminution of the one vital check on communications of all kinds – that is, feedback. Newspapers retain their letter columns, but letters seldom affect editorial policy in Britain, as the history of the Northcliffe and Beaverbrook empires should prove. Sales of newspapers reflect less the individual preference of readers for particular editorial values than the economics of newspaper production. Only big circulation newspapers can hope to attract sufficient advertising to enable them to survive. (Quality Sunday newspapers like the *Sunday Times* and *Observer* survive less on their circulation than their ability to reach the wealthy readerships classified as 'A–B', which enables them to charge high rates for advertising space. A low-circulation quality daily newspaper like *The Times*, even with advertising, runs at a heavy loss.) Feedback which affects a newspaper's editorial policy is therefore strictly limited.

Feedback from the British television audience to programme controllers, and which can affect editorial content, is even more limited. Take, for example, the growth in BBC sports programmes, which was based far more on the ideas of one programme controller (Paul Fox) than on any statistical justification which had charted viewers' choices. ITV's *Jictar* ratings system provides no feedback for viewers. The BBC panel system provides a limited feedback to programme controllers and producers. Dallas P. Smythe declares that the broadcasters 'are in effect autonomous, irresponsible except through their own conscience to the viewer, or listener'.

Enter McLuhan

Professor Marshall McLuhan, *enfant terrible* of communications theorists, has provided a radical assessment of the whole nature and methods of the media. Much in his writing is paradoxical, a joke in which trendiness and triviality, meaning and madness are mixed in a series of non-verifiable statements. Some would claim that his underlying analysis is intensely serious, and that it provides useful insights into the nature of the electronic challenge. Others would agree with the critic Raymond Williams that McLuhan's work is 'an apparently sophisticated technological determinism'.

In order to grasp even a small part of what McLuhan is trying to say, it is necessary to attempt to follow his ideas, which he chooses to express only in a highly individualistic way. For him 'the village had achieved a social and institutional extension of all human faculties'. What the present electronic media have done is to extend the boundary of man's village to encompass the whole globe. For McLuhan, the dictionary definition of a medium as being 'a way through which communication is maintained, a channel for information' is taken literally. The medium itself is the message, content is always another medium. If this seems nonsense, it is because the nature of McLuhan's task is difficult, because he wishes to awake in us a perception of a new kind of awareness. For him roads, transport, clocks and mathematical number-systems are also media; they too are extensions of our human faculties, of our physical and nervous systems. Furthermore, he claims that 'all media exist to invest our lives with artificial perception and arbitrary values'.

Life in the village or city-state once depended on oral communication. Literacy brought about detachment from the village, though against this loss came the invention of printing with its resultant accuracy, message-uniformity and repeatability. Mass production and mass printing followed, becoming increasingly interdependent, through advertising. Then came the inventions of electrical communication: telegraph, telephone, phonograph, radio, television and computers. Suddenly communications were altered in a fundamental way. Gone was the exclusiveness of the print-media, when man withdraws into private experience. The print media depended on old-fashioned methods of physical distribution. The new electronic media provide instant verbal and visual contact. Thanks to the electronic media, man once again lives in his village, now vastly extended.

McLuhan divided his media into 'hot' media and 'cool' media. Hot media are first of all those that extend the human senses 'in high definition'; that is, they provide plenty of data or detail. A photograph is 'hot' because it provides plenty of visual data, whereas a cartoon, providing very little, is 'cool'. Secondly, all hot media require low participation by the individual receiving the message, because all that is necessary is to receive the plentiful information provided. Hot media include the cinema (a moving photograph), radio and print – all technically efficient in communication.

In contrast, cool media require high participation or completion by the audience, because they only transmit in low definition. Secondly they relay relatively little content. Cool media include speech, telephone and television. McLuhan's explanation of this differentiation is that speech is cool, because so little information is given, and so much has to be filled in by the listener. The telephone is a cool medium of low definition because the ear is given a meagre portion of the voice print. Television is cool, because 'the television image is a mosaic mesh of light and dark spots' (which a movie shot never is, even when the quality of the movie image is very poor), so it demands attention to be decipherable. That is why television depends extensively on close-ups, since the quality of wide-shots is too indistinct on the cathode-ray tube.

Some critics have found inconsistencies in the McLuhan differentiation between the various types of electronic media. But his basic premise that the electronic media have brought a vast change in the nature of the influence of communications is widely accepted. He asks, 'What possible immunity can there be from the subliminal operation of a new medium like television? Television is above all an extension of the sense of touch. It is the total involvement in all-inclusive nowness that occurs in young lives via television's mosaic image.'

In plainer language, McLuhan believes that television has a range of effects that are entirely due to the immediate nature of watching the cathode-ray tube, irrespective of what we are watching. 'The medium is the message,' he said, and, equally tellingly, 'The medium is the massage.' Caught in its spell, we assimilate a range of messages quite apart from the intellectual content of the programme. There is no need for advertisers to attempt subliminal advertising, because the very nature of the television input gets past our conscious mental censor. The less literate the individual, the more total is the effect, hence the argument that children are more vulnerable than adults. Vulnerable to what, we ask? To 'all-inclusive nowness' – here McLuhan becomes delphic, asserting that we should withhold value-judgements when studying media matters, since their effects are not capable of being isolated. But he does believe that the all-persuasive influences of the electronic media can be resisted, by acquiring the antidote of related media like print. Television demands participation; the detached world of print can provide a defence mechanism based on a private determination to analyse rather than to participate. For McLuhan, education will become recognized as the Civil Defence against media fallout.[2]

McLuhan's critics

McLuhan's refusal to come to terms with contemporary criticism of the media by blandly denying that such criticism is even possible has raised considerable opposition. Content does matter. The content of television can vary from factual news to the publicizing of goods for sale, together with a range of pure entertainment programmes which in themselves imply value-judgements about the nature of possessions and the structure of our capitalist society. Programmes vary in quality from serious productions which can approach the status of art forms, to the more superficial series, and sometimes to complete triviality.

Most surveys of the medium have been exclusively concerned with the obvious questions about content. How persuasive can the mass media be on certain issues? Can the mass media help to solve some of our current world problems? Can they persuade us to act contrary to our better judgement? Should more government control be exercised over them? McLuhan would dismiss these questions. He wrote: 'The spokesmen of censorious views are typically semi-illiterate, book-orientated individuals who have no competence in the grammars of newspaper, or radio, or film, but who look askew and askance at all non-book media.'

McLuhan's emphasis on the revolutionary character of the non-book media is beginning to receive serious attention. Writers like Alan Hancock, now head of television at UNESCO Hawaii, agree that 'the effect of television is greater than the sum total of the programmes it transmits. The medium itself, the basic device of television, has effects and implications quite apart from its material'.[3] Hancock cites the effect of television viewing on family life. Does it hinder or assist the development of the family group? Television's effects on children and adolescents, on politics and belief is clearly greater than the sum of the content of individual programmes. Are the effects of television on our social and economic development capable of being differentiated from the effects of the other mass media?

Raymond Williams believes that such questions need rephrasing. 'Effects', he writes, 'can only be studied in relation to real intentions, and these will often have to be as distinguished from declared intentions as from assumed and indifferent general social processes.' But he believes that these approaches should be concerned with what he calls 'real agency', and that they can be valid within their own research terms. But McLuhan's theories he completely rejects as explicitly ideological – the culmination of an aesthetic theory that became a social theory in a negative sense. 'It is', Raymond Williams says, 'apparently sophisticated technological determinism which has the significant effect of indicating a social and cultural determinism.'

To put it more simply, Williams sees McLuhan as saying that if the media are the cause, then all the other causes which we lump together as history become reduced to mere effects of that cause. All other causes are irrelevant to the direct 'physiological and therefore "physic" effects of the media as such'.[4]

McLuhan's images – the 'electronics age' and the 'global village' – for example – Williams sees as emanating from his wholly unhistorical and asocial base, and as such ludicrous. His argument that 'the effect of the media is the same whoever controls or uses it, whatever be the apparent content', is an argument for letting technology run itself, making the political and cultural content of the media irrelevant. At this level, McLuhan is providing a glossy *avant-garde* theory for the crudest self-justifications of the media-men. McLuhan's theories would justify the claims of the IBA for the fourth television channel in their submissions to the government, and the 'monopoly of good judgement' which ex-BBC TV Head of Current Affairs Mrs Grace Wyndham Goldie claims for broadcasters in her lecture to the Society of Film and Television Arts.[5] Williams believes that the strange rhetoric of McLuhan's theory of communications is unlikely to last long. He sees it as significant only as 'the ideological representation of technology as a cause', and because there may be successors to his determinist beliefs. But McLuhan's essential position is already discredited. Meanwhile other sociologists have set out to discover whether television does alter attitudes.

Television and social evolution

In 1965 Political and Economic Planning (an independent body) set up a conference to study whether 'television programmes were having a substantial influence on civic thinking and action'. They detected various ground-swells in British life which included:

a. A growth of sceptical attitudes to advertisers, salesmen and manipulative persuaders. The rise of 'consumerism', as illustrated by the publication *Which*, and the television programmes which used its findings, contributed to this scepticism.

b. New ideas about the roles trade unionism should assume in relation to industry and the State. Increasingly newspapers and television industrial reporters looked more at the effects of strikes than at their underlying causes.

c. A widening of community ties, to extend beyond national frontiers. Regional television studios, Eurovision and finally satellite television made reporters in Paris and New York seem no further away than the newscaster in London. The Eurovision song contest with its audience of over one hundred million, contributed to the belief that all television audiences are, deep down, much the same.

d. A growth in permissive attitudes to personal morality. Television mirrors these changes, with the 'human' policemen in *Z Cars*, and a concern for personal and social problems in *Armchair Theatre*, the *Wednesday Play* and similar drama series, as well as in the many documentary series, including in particular *Man Alive*.

e. A considerable reduction in the social distance that had hitherto separated different categories of people. Television had always been interested in the rich since the days when Richard Dimbleby toured the great houses and the public schools. Now it became interested in the poor, and the socially inadequate. Television looked at abortion, homelessness and drunkenness, and at blacks, both at home and overseas, especially in America.

PEP concluded their report with a series of questions. They asked how television affected attitudes to civic culture; what were the distinctive characteristics of television in changing social attitudes; and what were the mechanisms that produce resistance or acceptance of changed norms.[6]

The power of the moving picture

Moving pictures had been used for trying to influence public thought and action since the second decade of the twentieth century. The 1914–18 War stimulated this use of the cinema. At the beginning of the war the English film journal *Bioscope* suggested that special films on the causes, meaning and appeal of the War should be prepared 'free from any suggestion of jingoism, bearing upon them the imprint of a simple, faithful rendering of facts'. It was a delightfully naive suggestion, since the cinematographic departments of all the warring nations were only interested in films which exalted their cause, and stimulated recruitment. The best newsreel of 1916, *The Battle of the Somme*, was both realistic and very effective propaganda for the War effort.

Lloyd George was the first Prime Minister to perceive the power of pictures. He said of *The Battle of the Somme* in a rhetorical phrase, 'Be up and doing. See that this picture, which is in itself an epic of self sacrifice and gallantry, reaches everyone. Herald the deeds of our brave men to the ends of the earth.' Films made a major contribution to the mythology of war. With newspapers and photographs, they provided the basis of the public's information.[7]

Feature films clumsily supplemented the propaganda of the newsreels. The Germans pictured barbarous Senegalese soldiers murdering German children in the cause of French civilization. French and English films portrayed the brutal Hun crushing Europe under his boot and shooting the civilian population. The Americans went further, featuring stars like Mary Pickford, a symbol of sweetness and innocence, as a near-victim of German rape and bestiality. In *Hearts of the World* Lillian Gish goes as far as to kill a German officer herself.

After the First World War film became widely recognized as a measurable instrument of propaganda. In the thirties the rise of Nazism produced films both for and against Nazism. By the Second World War it was found possible to make accurate assessments of the effects of film on United States servicemen. The United States Government took over the Jam Handy Company in Detroit to utilize their experience in making persuasion and training films for war propaganda. British, American and German studios played a major propaganda role in the Second World War.

Measuring the effects of television: content analysis

During the fifties 'content analysis' studies proliferated. The basis of these studies lay in trying to assess how some items of content, such as a politically persuasive advertisement, produced 'effects' like a change in voting intentions. The theory, dubbed the 'hypodermic theory', was that a viewer could be given a dose of a particular persuasion and his reactions analysed. However, though many attempts were made to assess this theory, the results were curiously negative.

As a result sociologists turned to an important variant of this theory, termed the 'tidal flow' theory. They realized increasingly that effect analysis was elusive. It became necessary to ask questions like 'Who? says what? in which channel? to whom? with what effect?' The answers could be conveniently grouped as Control Analysis, Content Analysis, Media Analysis, Audience and Effect Analysis. The sheer scale of television broadcasting makes this sort of analysis difficult, but the picture that emerges is instructive.

The 'tidal flow' model shows a flood of communication from media organizations past communicators designated 'gatekeepers', then out via the broadcasting network to small groups like families, which have within them their own 'gatekeeping' opinion leaders (for instance the father or mother). The flood of communication can be compared to the sea coming up a river delta, where the water will flow up different tributaries at different speeds, and will sometimes meet resistance. This resistance is not always easy to assess, and is different from the feedback that comes from telephone calls in protest, or in letters of complaint. The communications flood is itself made up of many different strands – not only from television, films and the press, but also from opinion leaders who find many different ways of communicating their opinions.

Content analysis, as formulated in 'Who says what, how, to whom, with what effect?' leaves out the whole question of *intention*. If we added the question 'for what purpose?' we might learn more about the agencies of communication and their interests. So far sociologists working with the assumptions and methods of the 'sociology of mass communications' can tell us sociological truths – for instance that 'television is a factor in socialization' ('socialization' being defined as 'learning the ways and becoming a functioning member of society'). But this is to say very little until we know more about how the forms of society affect the functions of communications and their controls.

The power of television compared with other media

Research has shown that one of the main effects of the media is their tendency to reinforce each other and to emphasize the same values. Television seems to have an increasingly powerful influence over public thought and action. Whereas formerly newspapers were the main force influencing public attitudes, with radio and television reinforcing them, now the pattern is reversed and television is the most important single influence.[8]

An ITA survey in 1966 showed that 48 per cent of television set owners relied more on television than on the newspapers for news, 29 per cent relied equally on both, and 23 per cent relied more on the press. The explanation would seem to lie in the fact that moving pictures on television make news more comprehensive and more convincing.[9]

We cannot yet measure precisely television's effect on changing social attitudes. Social changes happen too slowly. Does television lead or reflect? Measurement must also take into account the social and psychological variables of the viewer which influence reaction to any programme. Television programmes do often appear to reflect evolving attitudes on social issues such as capital punishment, comprehensive education, and homelessness – often sooner and more accurately than the print media. Sometimes tele-

vision appears to be leading the way with a single programme like *Cathy Come Home*. However, appearances
can be deceiving. *Cathy Come Home* was but one of many
programmes about housing and homelessness that had
been broadcast over a period as a reflection of the worries
and fears of many social workers in the field. Perhaps all
we can conclude from the evidence so far cited is that television programmes can signal the slow emergence of a new
consciousness. They are highly unlikely to produce a sudden change in belief and attitudes comparable to Paul's
vision on the road to Damascus.

Chapter Nine

Cassettes, Cable and Satellites

Television technology, like all technologies, will not remain static. Nothing very startling may have happened in the last twenty years of television transmission, apart from the introduction of colour and the cautious welcome given to satellite hook-ups. But three major revolutions are waiting in the wings, ready to be brought on when sufficient investment and a cue from the tele-communication authorities permit. Of the three, the video-cassette is the least dramatic. The cable revolution could bring enormous changes to television broadcasting – and satellite transmissions could transform television reception in the third world.

Video-cassettes have been talked about since 1968 without anything much being done. The challenge to record television programmes goes back to the early fifties, when recordings were achieved with the use of a 35mm or 16mm film camera. These so-called *Kines* were of poor quality, and required film laboratory treatment before they could be transmitted. Clearly some video replica of the highly-adaptable sound tape-recorder was the answer, and Ampex came up with their first commercially viable videotape recorder based on the 'quadriplex' method of tape scanning. They were expensive – £20,000 was too much for schools and colleges to pay. The BBC had already invented its own system called VERA but it was enormously expensive on tape and the project was abandoned. Then came the invention of the helical scan video-tape recorder which was much cheaper, if of inferior quality. Soon a variety of tape standards and widths appeared on the market, generally mutually incompatible, but tape remained expensive at about £25 for half-an-hour's worth, and the machines remained complex to operate.

What was needed was a simple recording and playback device which operated on the colour standard, and which would be cheap enough to make home purchase possible. A variety of companies including the EVR/CBS consortium, Philips, Sony and others announced plans during 1968 and 1969. I remember attending the first video-cassette conference VIDCA in 1971 in Cannes, where the air was thick with bigger and better claims made by the different manufacturers, all producing mutually incompatible systems. First in the field was EVR, an adaptation of an 8mm film system, electronically scanned. It worked well in black and white, but there were delays in introducing the colour system. Its two great drawbacks were that it could not record, and that the manufacture of EVR cassettes could only be done at the EVR plants in the United States, Britain and Japan at prices that the consortium chose to impose.

There were long delays in getting these plants fully operational, and during the delay electronics companies like Sony, Admiral and Philips caught up. Their machines could record off-air transmissions. Philips machines are also fitted with a clock, so that you can record your favourite programme while you are out; they are now being bought in large quantities in Britain by education authorities. They were about the same price as EVR machines – around £400. The only thing EVR could do and they could not was hold a still picture for classroom instruction. The most technically advanced of all was the RCA *selectavision* machine, based on the principle of laser holography. But RCA never managed to produce a production-line model.

Research continues. Videodiscs are also in the laboratory phase. They may well prove to be the most economical answer to the problem of recording television programmes. Supporters of the older 8mm film still abound, led, not surprisingly, by Kodak, who manufacture most of the 8mm film stock. Inside the educational world, 8mm silent film loops have been popular for some years, and now 8mm sound projectors with cassetted film are also available, sometimes at half the cost of video-cassette players. Interestingly the Open University chose to use this method of offering playback possibilities to those students who needed to see programmes in the local situation instead of when transmitted. However the quality of the video-cassette to 8mm transfer process was often inferior. The old-fashioned technologies cannot be expected to match the greater picture clarity of the new electronic systems.

Why has the video-cassette 'revolution' never really happened? Two reasons are clear. In the first place the manufacturers promised machines earlier than they could in fact produce them. Robert Heron, Programme Director of the EVR partnership once wrote in glowing terms: 'One would not need to be an intrepid adventurer to suggest that the significance of the television cassette for at least a decade or two ahead is considerable, perhaps astronomical . . . With the ease of taking a paperback from a shelf or a record from a rack, the cassette destroys once and for all the one-way communication track of the runaway hardware, and a dialogue can begin. One of the early advantages lies in the sector of data-storage and information-retrieval. If education is, in fact, to become enquiry-based, if the learner is to have wide-ranging access to the audio-visual repertoire now undeniably under-utilized, the television cassette provides a practical vehicle.'[1] But his company's translation of such hopes into reality was constantly postponed, until eventually the processing plant at Basildon in Essex was packed up and sent to Japan.

The second reason is that the price breakthrough promised by the manufacturers never happened. The cost of the player is less important than the cost of the tape or film cassettes in their unrecorded state. The cost of half an hour's 16mm colour film is at least £60 in 1976. The equivalent price of video or EVR should have been a quarter of that. In fact it turned out to be nearly one half of the cost, which was not nearly so attractive.

There is no doubt that the video-cassette revolution will

in fact materialize. What is in doubt is how the invention will be utilized. One possible way might be through video-cassette lending libraries. W. H. Smith, the nationally-known stationers, have set up a company to create such libraries. Distribution might be by wire. Viewers would simply ring a local number in order to have a cassette programme piped into their sets. But before that can happen television by cable has to become much more common than it is at present. At the moment cable television is not permitted to carry any other programmes than those transmitted by the BBC and ITV – the only exceptions are the five cable companies described below.

Cable television – bottled-up genii?

Cable television had humble beginnings; the cable was just an easy way round the problems of poor reception. It all began when in 1949 the wife of Mr L. E. Parsons, a radio station operator in Astoria, Oregon, wanted to watch television beamed from Seattle, Washington, which was 125 miles away. By putting up an antenna fifty feet high he found he could get good reception. Soon he was supplying signal feeds to other local residents at one hundred dollars a feed. Community Antennae Television (CATV) as it is still often called began to catch on wherever reception was difficult. CATV became as popular in big cities as it was in country areas. From a mere 14,000 CATV subscribers in 1952, the number has risen to 5.3 million. The National Cable Television Association of America predicts that it could have between twenty-five and thirty-two million subscribers by 1980.

The excitement produced by CATV arises from its capacity to carry a very large number of different channels at the same time. From five to twelve different signals is the current American average, but in a few places it carries twenty-seven channels, and systems with forty to sixty channels are on the way. This ability opens the way to local programming, hitherto prohibited. It also opens the way to amateur access to television, because the cost is low, and the audience local. Imagine a monthly programme for

Afghan-hound owners – a specialist subject, but perfectly reasonable when there are channels to spare. And of course spare channels are already being used by CATV channels to cover stock-market trends, weather-maps and public announcements. In the future cable could be used to print newspaper bulletins in the subscriber's house, and even to act as a computer terminal. As Brenda Maddox wrote in her book *Beyond Babel*: 'Cable television is almost too good to be true, a *deus ex machina* to rout the McLuha-nites. The medium of television need no longer be the message; it can be split into dozens of different kinds of messages, some visual, some printed, some personal, some even international if satellites are joined to cable ter-minals.'[2]

Turning to more immediate possibilities, cable could immediately cut the cost of appearing on television for American politicians. The cost of an hour's time on a cable channel might be as little as thirty dollars. At present the cost of appearing on American commercial television is very high, and, worse still, many of the listeners are not in the right area, and so unable to vote for the candidate any-way. There is considerable waste of air-waves when a can-didate from a small congressional district in New York City sprays his message all over northern New Jersey and south-western Connecticut. Of course, in non-democratic countries there could be a more sinister aspect of cable television's ability to create special audiences. In South Africa for instance it would be possible to wire black town-ships to receive totally different programmes from those received by the white suburbs. And if all sets were only able to receive cable signals, then no signals from overseas transmitted by overhead satellite would be receivable by cable viewers.

Cable television in the United States was for years in danger of being strangled by the telephone companies be-cause they were operating in competing areas. Then in 1968 the Supreme Court suddenly ruled that cable tele-vision was under the control of the Federal Communica-tions Commission, and that re-transmission of a television broadcast did not constitute a performance according to the law of American copyright. Therefore the cable companies began to act as broadcasters instead of wiring companies under State law. The FCC ruled that cable operators not only could, but in time should, originate programmes of their own. They could sell commercial advertising if they wished. And the FCC began to attack the stranglehold on cable systems sought by the telephone companies.

In 1971 progress was slowed by President Nixon, determined to protect network broadcasting of NBC, CBS and ABC. Whilst cable companies could import signals from other stations into big cities, they had to pay copyright on the films they took 'out of the air', and they were not to import programmes on which a local station had bought exclusive rights. There is little chance of the cable systems becoming a fourth television network in the United States in the forseeable future. But at least in the United States people are excited by cable, seeing it, correctly, as potentially a great new public service similar to the telephone system but commercially owned.

Cable television in Britain

Already about 7 per cent of British licence holders subscribe to cable television companies or, as they are known in the UK, wired television or television relay. This is about the same proportion as the United States, but far behind Canada which is 25 per cent cable. The areas in Britain so far covered are parts of central London, and parts of Newcastle, Hull, Sheffield, Leeds, Bristol, Wellingborough and Swindon, plus the valleys of South Wales and other areas where reception is poor. The older circuits consist of two wires to every house, like a telephone system. This does not offer much scope for expansion. But the newer systems use co-axial cables as in Canada and the USA, and they could easily carry multiple systems. In past years there have been battles with the Post Office which has only licensed them for brief periods of the order of three years.

In 1966 came the first attempt in Britain to set up a cable television station, with the introduction of Pay TV Ltd, a company using British Relay wires, in parts of London and Sheffield. The experiment involved the supply of special programmes which could be obtained as long as coins were placed in the box attached to the set. These special programmes were mainly films and sporting events, but only 10,000 people took part in the experiment. In 1968 the Labour Government refused to allow the experiment to expand, because of ideological objections to private broadcasting, so the exercise was terminated with Pay TV losing around a million pounds.

With the return of the Conservatives a far more interesting experiment began – community television. In 1972, using the existing wired networks, small companies were licensed to start their own local television programmes in Greenwich, Swindon, Sheffield, Bristol and Wellingborough. No charges for this service were permitted, so it was very much a venture in faith for the companies, who risked the necessary funds in the hope that eventually they would be granted a licence to operate commercially. The stations that I have seen have produced some enormously exciting programming – completely local, and totally different from anything shown on network or regional television in Britain to date.

To quote one example, the handout for Bristol Channel Cablevision claimed: 'Bristol Channel is yours, more yours than any television you've ever seen. If you prefer not just sitting there – come to Broad Plain (their studio) and appear on television, make the programme yourself, operate the equipment. This equipment is specially designed for the public to use. Camera, lighting, sound, if that's what interests you, come and use it.' Plenty of people with no previous experience seemed ready and anxious to take the station at its word. Volunteers borrowed portable video-recorders, went off to shoot local events like a show or a bowling match, and returned to edit and transmit it themselves. Community television really is access television in the true sense of the word. Anyone who wants to raise an issue has a reasonable chance of getting on the screen.

The licences for these cable experiments lasted only three years. The companies had to seek the written permission of the Minister of Posts and Telecommunications before they transmitted. During the day the companies provided the normal network services from BBC 1, BBC 2 and ITV; in the evenings for an hour or more there was a locally-originated programme. At weekends there was very much more broadcasting. Every station had different hours, and Bristol was keen on a morning broadcast too. But the return of a Labour Government did not encourage the cablevision companies. They felt it unlikely that such a government would allow them what they really wanted – a handsome revenue from local advertising. Other objections to such a development of local cablevision came not only from local newspapers which depend on local advertising but also from radical groups, which feel that this new communications opportunity should not be given to the sort of commercial interests which run ITV. Prohibited from advertising, the experimental stations were all abandoned as financially unviable, though the Greenwich service survives in a different form.

Another development which will be studied by the Annan Committee is *dial-a-programme*, developed by the British relay company Rediffusion. Since this system depends not on co-axial cables, but on simple telephone-type wires, it provides programmes from a central programme-exchange rather like a telephone exchange. The viewer dials a code which provides instructions indicating what tape is to be played to his screen. When he wants to change channels, the viewer only has to press a button which will then produce a visual display of the other programmes available and their codes.

Implications of cable technology

If cable is proposed for Britain, three reactions can be predicted. First, the BBC will immediately make an official protest. It has always been monopolist in outlook, and considers that any extension of choice outside its own two channels would result in the fragmentation of broadcasting resources, with a consequent decline in quality. There is good evidence for this view.

It is sad but true that the best financed companies in the United States are offering their own version of the worst of broadcasting – an unlimited diet of old films, old cartoons and bad variety.

Secondly, it will be claimed that the introduction of cable television would strike at the principle of equality of reception–opportunity for all viewers. Both BBC and IBA have spent vast sums in trying to ensure that nearly every part of the British Isles receives a good television signal. As Sir Charles Curran, Director-General of the BBC, put it, 'So far, there has been general assent on the proposition that broadcasting financed by the public should serve all the public.' Against his view it could be argued that cable television is no more unfair to the public than BBC local radio, which is supported by the licence fees, but which is not available to a large section of the population.

Thirdly, cable will be opposed by the existing ITV companies, particularly if they think that the introduction of cable would prevent the introduction of a second channel for ITV. All existing ITV companies have spent large sums of money on studios and equipment. They cannot be expected to welcome other commercial television competitors who can offer cheaper advertising rates to manufacturers because their expenditure is so much less.

Once cable has been introduced, two further effects may result. First, cable companies are most unlikely to compete with each other, since no viewer is likely to subscribe to more than one company; so each cable company is likely to have its own local monopoly. As far as equality of access is concerned, even within cities, cable companies are unlikely to give complete coverage. Studies by the Rand Corporation in America have shown that high profits can be earned on a 40 per cent coverage with a relatively high subscription, and lowering the subscription and widening the coverage decreases profitability. This effectively discourages responsibility towards the general public.

The second effect of a successful introduction of cable might be to put pressure on the government to abandon the statutory licence fee whose proceeds benefit the BBC exclusively. Some governments might find it hard to resist the argument that the twin forces of commercial television on the network, and commercial radio at the local level catered well enough for all tastes, and that the statutory BBC licence fee was anomalous. The BBC is more vulnerable than it looks. Without sufficient revenue to ensure the quality of its programmes it could quickly lose its audience, and so part of the justification for its existence.

If Britain avoids the worst of the problems of untrammelled advertising that some parts of the United States has suffered, perhaps there is hope for the introduction of a responsible cable service of a different kind, genuinely run by, and serving, local communities. Given access to a full range of local affairs programmes for which the necessary resources had been specifically provided, perhaps by a local authority, cable could democratize broadcasting. The current argument about the need for democracy, for local television caring about local needs, for freedom of reception and access, is an argument in favour of legalizing and encouraging cable. Cable could cut down the power of typically remote and centralized broadcasting corporations, dependent as they are and must be on large capital investment. The democratic argument will doubtless be used by the big commercial companies advocating cable, while hoping for consumer-penetration under the cloak of community service. Purists like Professor Raymond Williams cannot conceive of a happy marriage between local community and commercial interests, and the example of California justifies such scepticism. So far, however, I have been most impressed by what the small cablevision companies in the United Kingdom have achieved with very little money, and no commercial income. The example of local radio, both BBC and commercial, is also encouraging.

Satellite broadcasting – messages from outer space

Communication satellites remain a miracle to those who accept television as an integral part of their everyday world. Communication satellites travel 22,300 miles above the equator, almost equidistant from every country and every person within their fantastic range. Only three satellites are necessary, theoretically, to make a single television audience out of the whole world. The satellite has caused some writers to wax lyrical: 'so small and so high, it seems to vault over the past, over mountains and oceans, and invites the whole world, jungle and suburb, to speak through it'.[3]

Satellites are a development in space of the micro-wave relay towers that dot the landscape, the most famous English one being the Post Office Tower in Central London. Satellites can receive and transmit simultaneously a large number of signals – including telephone, television, telex, photo-facsimile and computer-data. Instead of the old route-patterns which could mean that South American countries calling each other might have to route their calls through London, any country with a ground receiving station can transmit and receive satellite feeds – be it for telephone, television or any other electronic message system.

So far it is not possible to use a satellite to broadcast from space directly into a domestic television set. The transatlantic and transpacific satellite television feeds need ground stations at either end which receive and enormously amplify the signals before feeding them into the ordinary networks. A development has been the distribution satellite, which feeds medium-sized ground stations; this can be a cheaper distribution method than the older landlines. (An experiment along these lines has just started in India.) When we finally achieve direct reception from space there will be three possible ways to receive it: first through large 'community receivers', specially designed and placed in, say, the village square, for all to view. Next is the 'augmented' television set which has special equipment in order to tune in to a satellite. And third and far-thest in the future is the 'unaugmented' television set, which requires no special extra equipment to tune into space-originated signals.

Uses and abuses of satellite television

Not everybody has welcomed the opportunity to receive broadcasts from anywhere in the world. A United States congressman hailed the idea with the words, 'Maybe the citizen of the world has a right to choose what broadcasts he wants to listen to without national interference.' That sounded OK to him as an American. If however you are a citizen of the Third World, like the Argentinian Edgaro Galli, it sounds different. In May 1970 he wrote, 'The possibility of broadcasting to vast multinational regions entails the possibility that some of the countries in the area may receive educational or other programmes which do not take their true interests into consideration, or which may even exert a harmful cultural influence or some form of ideological pressure, thereby infringing the sovereignty of some or all of the countries in the region.'[4] He was not the first to express alarm at unrestricted global television. As early as 1963 the French proposed a ban on all broad-casting from space at the World Administrative Radio Conference of the ITU (International Telecommunications Union). Russia was also worried, and proposed that no broadcast should be sent into a country without the con-sent of its government.

Present technology only permits broadcasts to be aimed at a limited area, and educational subjects are the best to transmit over these areas. Of the various plans, only the Indian experiment is far developed. The Indian plan is to beam programmes into space from the Indian Earth Sta-tion at Ahmedabad which would then be beamed back to 5,000 villages each equipped with community receivers. Out of this experimental project designated SITE (Satel-lite Instructional Television Experiment) could grow the world's first all-satellite system, distributing television pro-grammes to half-a-million villages, teaching them about agriculture, literacy, nutrition and birth control. The United States' National Aerospace Agency (NASA) launched the first satellite for India, but future satellites will be Indian-launched. All the ground equipment is Indian-manufactured.

Of the 5,000 villages, 2,000 selected for their remoteness will receive their signals direct from space. Their receiving sets will, hopefully, cost around £30 with another £40 for the necessary converter.

Brazil, and a consortium of other Latin American countries would also like educational satellites and NASA has promised to launch one for them. Satellites provide a particularly dramatic solution to the problem of mass education. But their educational as opposed to technical success is still unproven, and warning voices are being raised. Dr Wilbur Schramm, Director of the Institute for Communication Research at Stanford University, California, said, 'If a country hurries into satellite communication without adequate preparation, it is likely to find itself making false steps, wasting resources, and risking a failure when and if it actually comes to the satellite stage.'

Only two nations have the resources to mount a global satellite service – the United States and Russia – and they are likely to agree that national sovereignty includes the right to refuse beamed satellite signals. But smaller nations, already finding the cost of running their own local television station expensive, might look on a free satellite input as irresistible, and so would painlessly import the products of a dominant commercial culture. The chief beneficiaries financially would be the big multi-national corporations who would find satellite-originated sponsored programmes the cheapest and most effective advertising medium open to them.

Hiding behind the phrase 'open skies', big corporations and authoritarian governments could dominate transmission, speaking to many nations who through poverty have little chance either to answer back, or to develop in defence their own national cultures through their own national and local broadcasting. Already satellites are owned by international bodies like INTELSAT, controlled mainly by the American COMSAT; and INTERSPUTNIK controlled by Russia (though INTERSPUTNIK technology lags behind). ESA, the European Space Agency, hopes to put up a communications satellite in due course. International agreement is urgently needed to prevent abuse of a system that has remarkable potential for good or evil in the future.

Other technological developments

New types of television receivers with large screens will, when introduced, strengthen the existing network companies, which will then produce the more spectacular programmes suited to the large screen. Equally, the expense may encourage Pay TV companies to provide special sporting events only available to large-screen subscribers of a wired service. They could additionally provide first-run feature films by direct on-the-spot payment through a meter.

Cable television, quite apart from providing programmes, could be used for shopping services, with a telephone system added; goods could be inspected and then ordered by television. It could also provide not just educational video-cassette hire, but also 'demand' information services for libraries and banks. As well as the print-out of a daily television-transmitted newspaper, cable television could also give 'telefax' or 'homofax' reproduction of a variety of printed material. These services, grouped under the general heading of 'Visual Information Services', could be either commercially or publicly owned – and ownership would vitally affect their usage and range of choice they offered.

Video-tape equipment, already a rich man's toy and some teachers' delight, offers remarkable opportunities for local programme-making by communities and schools. The work of groups such as Interaction in London's North Kensington offers high hopes of wider access to the television screen.

Finally, mention should be made of what are called 'reactive and interactive devices' – that is machines which provide the possibility of feedback. True community television could help to solve the problems of urban information flow, prevent civic alienation, and encourage democratic discussion, decision-making, and enhance community awareness. Voting by 'feedback' television has actual possibilities already, but the politicians are cautious. Advertisers are enormously interested in the possibilities of persuasion aimed at reactive consumers, since it would make market research easier and more accurate.

With so many radical developments in communication, there has never been a better time than the present for considering the whole of our communications structure. The old argument between 'public service' and 'commercial' broadcasting seems simple in comparison with the complex new choices raised by new opportunities. 'Public service' broadcasting can now mean much more than the Pilkington Committee of 1960 ever dreamed. No longer must we be concerned only with the traditional kind of centrally appointed authorities, whose Board of Governors may no longer perform its role as guardian of the public interest. Now 'public interest' can be interpreted democratically at the local level by local communities. As to the national broadcasting organizations; those who work in them, those who contribute occasionally, and those who receive their programmes, should equally participate in their control.

There is a danger that public service institutions may be swallowed by international commercial companies unless they can become more democratic and experimental. While we need central networking and programme provision, at the same time far more people should be able to have access to the channels of transmission. The old monopoly rights of the BBC and ITV programme makers must go. With public ownership of the means of transmission and studio production, outside production companies and individuals would have a reasonable opportunity to contribute. The huge 'creative' teams inside television today – in drama and light entertainment for example – could be broken down into groups competing with their ideas and their creativity. Cable companies and local film and television production companies could work hand in hand, with the chance of winning national transmission for their best offerings. A talented local man could find it easier to make the 'big time'.

Satellite television could protect cable and community television from insularity, and the nationalistic bias that from time to time creeps into our programming. Multinational programmes need not all sink to the bland nothingness of the Eurovision song contest. By retaining national characteristics they can help to explain one nation to another. Within the next few years decisions will have to be taken which will vitally affect the pattern of communications for our children and grandchildren. The battles and interactions between public service and commercial, between local, national and international broadcasting stations, between cable and broadcast signals, have been healthy and exciting. But quality is elusive and most often escapes when the first aim of communication is not to inform or entertain but to sell. Therefore new forms of democratic control will have to be found.

Chapter Ten

Control and Censorship – Limitations for Broadcasters

'Television . . . has created a fantasy world of visual dreams, and invested it with a greater authority of "reality" than the world a person experiences away from the television screen. And this new fantasy world is one where no moral order obtains, where such words as "good" and "evil" have no meaning, and "love" is reduced, in the jargon of the Schools Broadcasting Council in association with the BBC, to an "intercourse frame". It is a fantasy world coarsened by the camera's insensitive eye prying into scenes of cruelty, violence and death from which our human senses otherwise shrink. Thus we have the filming of public assassinations and executions, as well as of the very last moments of a human being's life in for instance films about hospitals or about Bangladesh. Also of accidents and shootings, when the lens is pushed as close as possible to the victim's dead face, if necessary tearing away the covering which others, with a natural feeling of respect, have placed over it. What is this but a form of visual blasphemy? Likewise when television parades sex and sexual attitudes, holding the camera in the closest possible proximity to fleshly intimacies, actual or simulated, without any regard for man's natural discretion. Such portrayals of sexual behaviour on television are contrary to normal experience and a menace to family life, superseding, as they do, the authority of parents by that of the screen's visual fantasy.'[1]

Television in Britain is under attack. As outlined in Chapter One, the main spearhead of the protest against sex and violence on British television screens came from the

National Viewers' and Listeners' Association and its sympathizers from the early sixties. Concern about misrepresentation and injustice to individuals came later, and led to the setting up of complaints commissions and increased interference on the part of BBC Governors in the teeth of opposition from the BBC Board of Management. No such victory was accorded to those concerned with sex and violence, yet it seems clear that the old permissiveness of the Greene regime of the early sixties has gone for ever. Control or censorship – today as never before these questions are being fought over by all who are concerned with broadcasting – politicians, programme makers and viewers. The long-term answers have yet to emerge. The Annan Committee may shed some light, but few can expect that broadcasters' 'freedoms' will escape entirely unscathed.

The moral protesters

Professor Richard Hoggart identified the forces of religious, moral and Christian protest as 'the new populists'. By no means a neutral witness, being not only a member of the General Advisory Council of the BBC, but also leader of *Track*, the anti-'Clean-Up Television' group, Hoggart claimed that the 'new populists' under the guise of protesting about dirt, gratuitous sex and excessive violence were in fact the new would-be censors. The charge of 'censorship' was so strongly made that it is worth probing the origins of the Clean-Up TV movement.

The first formal evidence of protest came with a meeting called at the Birmingham Town Hall on 5 May 1964. Organized by an energetic mother of three and teacher, Mrs Mary Whitehouse, this meeting quickly captured the headlines. 'Mothers Campaign for Higher TV Morals' was the front-page headline of the *Birmingham Mail*. Memories of *That Was The Week That Was* were still fresh, and the meeting agreed unanimously to ask the Chairman of the Governors of the BBC, Lord Normanbrook, to receive a deputation. The request was refused, and no official contact between the BBC and Mrs Whitehouse occurred until after Lord Normanbrook's death. Lord Hill, then Chairman of the ITA, did agree to see her, and repeated the invitation when he was appointed Chairman of the BBC governors. But this is to anticipate.

Whatever the BBC might make of Mrs Whitehouse, her cause found considerable support. Within twelve months James Dance MP presented a petition to Parliament signed by 365,355 people which stated the following: 'To: The Honourable the Commons of the United Kingdom of Great Britain and Northern Ireland in Parliament assembled: The humble Petition of residents of Bromsgrove and other places showeth that on the walls of Broadcasting House is carved – "This temple of the Arts and Muses is dedicated to Almighty God by the first Governors of Broadcasting. It is their prayer that all things hostile to peace and purity be banished from this house and that the people inclining their ear to whatsoever things are beautiful and honest and of good report may tread the paths of wisdom and righteousness." That the men and women of Great Britain believe in a Christian way of life; deplore present day attempts to belittle and destroy it, and in particular object to the propaganda of disbelief, doubt and dirt that the BBC pours into millions of homes through the television screen; and that crime, violence and illegitimacy and venereal disease are steadily increasing, yet the BBC employs people whose ideas and advice pander to the lowest in human nature, accompanying this with a stream of suggestive and erotic plays which present promiscuity, infidelity and drinking as normal and inevitable. Wherefore your petitioners pray that the BBC be asked to make a radical change of policy and produce programmes which build character instead of destroying it, which encourage and sustain faith in God, and bring Him back to the heart of the British family and national life.'

The petition accurately translates from the original Latin the inscription that Lord Reith had placed in the foyer of Broadcasting House in 1935. In the intervening years the attitudes both in broadcasting and in society had changed tremendously, but the petitioners felt confident enough to state 'that the men and women of Great Britain believe in a Christian way of life'. And they had justification for thinking that the BBC did so too – the BBC launched its second channel with a splendid dedicatory service in Westminster Abbey, which was of course broadcast. One of the prayers might have been written by the Clean-Up TV campaign itself: 'Grant we beseech thee, O Almighty God, to all to whom is committed the responsibility of broadcasting, such a hearing of Thy Word of Truth that others hearing it through them may apprehend; and such a Vision of Beauty that others seeing it through them may understand; make them sensitive to Thy Word and obedient to the Vision; and so unite their skills of brain and hand with a sense of service to their fellow men that they may do their part in making the heart of the people wise, its thinking sound, and its will righteous, to Thy greater glory, Father, Son and Holy Spirit, God blessed for evermore. Amen.'

Clearly there was a degree of schizophrenia between the BBC's official position and what it actually produced. Perhaps it might have been more honest to announce officially that the influence of Lord Reith was finally dead. For whatever the prayers had hoped for, there was no sign on BBC 2 Sunday night drama that producers were much concerned with the 'Vision of Beauty'. The *Daily Express* wrote: 'A heretic seared with a cross-shaped branding iron ... French revolutionaries taking reprisals after a peasants' revolt by desecrating a church and ravishing a young girl on an altar – such is the new, brutal-look BBC's Channel 2 ... Sunday plays will shock – the scenes are vivid and uncensored.' The *Sunday Telegraph* on 25 May was even more specific: 'The final casualty list in Ken Taylor's trilogy on man and belief for BBC 2 *The Seekers* was one bayoneting, one crushing under a jackboot, one beard set on fire, one suicide by intravenous injection, one rape, one flogging, and six brandings with a cruciform iron. Who says now that BBC 2 offers nothing different?' Critics rallied to the BBC's defence, but by no means all of them. What had begun as a grass-roots protest became a powerful movement led by MPs like James Dance and up to one hundred colleagues, and supported by bishops led by the Bishop of Hereford, and including the then Archbishop of York.

In the *BBC Handbook* for 1966 official recognition was given to the controversy in the form of an eight-page section entitled 'BBC – Focus of Controversy'. This balanced major attacks on the Corporation with contrasting quotations from its supporters. The article cited the Church of Scotland report on 'The New Impuritans', which accused the BBC of a 'definite attempt to impose upon the public the standards and values and points of view on religion and morals that are held by a minority'.

This was contrasted with Ian James of the *Catholic Herald* who stated that 'it is a positive duty for the BBC to put on programmes which shock, disturb and anger'. If that were true, the BBC continued to do its duty. 1966 became a crucial year, with the first convention of the protest movement, which was now renamed the National Viewers' and Listeners' Association. The previous December, Mr Sydney Newman, Head of BBC Drama, had issued a warning to his staff about the treatment of sex and religion in plays. But judging by the amount of evidence collected by the NVALA, as they called themselves, few producers and directors had taken the hint.

The new Chairman of the BBC's Governors, Lord Hill, made it clear when he met Mrs Whitehouse, James Dance MP, the chairman of NVALA, and one other on 9 November 1967 that 'no organization would have a special position in relation to the BBC, though her organization was entitled to have its views considered as well as any others'.[2] Although this appeared to be a rebuff, subsequent events were to prove that Lord Hill was sensitive to the NVALA campaign, and was to do much to strengthen the Governors' control of the Director-General and the Executive. In his own words he 'treated Mrs Whitehouse and her colleagues with care, recognizing that the central theme of her campaign could not be contemptuously dismissed'.[3]

The doctor's medicine: strengthen the governors

Lord Hill's chairmanship of the BBC will long be remembered. He was the first Chairman of the BBC in history to modify the power of the Board of Management. More important still, he was the first Chairman to try to curb a Director-General and win. Until Lord Hill's appointment, Sir Hugh Greene had been able to ride over criticism with very little difficulty. He told a BBC meeting on 13 November 1963 that even if the government had viewed his appointment 'with the utmost distaste, there was nothing they could do about it'. Later, at Middlesbrough, he assured his audience that 'we have never taken into account any notice of minority groups and the Governors are beginning to ignore them as well'.[4] This statement hardly accords with Paragraph 15 of the BBC Charter which speaks of the need to 'bring the work of the Corporation under constant and effective review from without' and to 'provide suitable and sufficient means for the presentation to the Corporation ... of criticism and suggestions so represented'.

Lord Hill's transfer from the ITA to the BBC in July 1967 produced a rash of press headlines. 'Anger at the BBC Over Lord Hill Takeover' announced the *Sketch*. Others included 'Just How Tough Will Lord Hill get with Alf Garnett?' 'Consultant or Sawbones?' and 'Is This The Politicians' Revenge?' All these headlines hinted at aspects of the truth, but Lord Hill was to prove too independent a thinker to yield to any one pressure group, inside the BBC or outside it.

The role of the governors was changing. Under Reith, who had experienced considerable conflict with the first Chairman, Lord Clarendon, and with one of the Governors, Mrs Philip Snowden, a document had been produced which prevented effective interference by the governors. Drawn up by the second Chairman, J. H. Whitley, it was shown to each of the incoming governors, who agreed to discuss and decide major matters of policy and finance with the Director-General, and then to leave the execution of policy to him and his 'competent officers'.

This position was altered by the Labour Government *White Paper* of 1946. The Commons debate following its publication led to the Lord President of the Council saying: 'I have heard the theory advanced that the set-up of the BBC provides that the Director-General runs the undertaking and that the Governors act as a kind of consultative body . . . it is a wrong doctrine. The Governors are the BBC. They are solely responsible for its working, and the Director-General and his staff are subject to their orders and directions, which the Governors are free to pass.'[6] Five years later, in its reaction to the *Beveridge Report*, the Labour Government 'saw no reason to dissent from the views of the Committee that the Whitley document should disappear'.[7] But old habits die hard. Soon after Barbara Wootton was appointed a governor she asked Sir William Haley how he conceived the function of the governors. 'I look on them as a reserve of wisdom.' To which Barbara Wootton replied, 'Like the gold reserve of the Bank of England, I suppose, not to be drawn upon.'[8]

The arrival of the Independent Television Authority, with its own policy-making structure tied to a Board of Governors, encouraged the BBC governors to take on additional roles. While they still attempted to govern and criticize the functioning of the BBC from the standpoint of lay members of the public, they also felt responsible for ultimate decisions on behalf of their Corporation which was now in desperate competition with another similar enterprise. Lord Hill at the ITA and Lord Normanbrook began to have quiet informal meetings every other month at which no other governors were present.

Lord Normanbrook attracted a lot of press criticism when, acting on his own, he decided not to renew an invitation to Mr Ian Smith to appear in the late-night current affairs programme *24 Hours*. Later, in one of the BBC lunchtime lectures, Lord Normanbrook chose to defend his actions like this: 'I am not here concerned to argue whether that decision was right or wrong. I am concerned only with my right to make it. In some quarters my decision was represented as an "intervention"; and one of the weekly periodicals took this further by asking why I should feel that as Chairman I had "the power to make essentially executive decisions" . . . These interpretations show a complete misunderstanding of the constitutional position of the Board of Governors and their Chairman. The Board is, in fact, an integral part of the BBC: it is the final source of decision, not only on general policy, but on specific issues which are of sufficient importance to call for decisions at the highest level within the Corporation . . . No producer enjoys an absolute and unlimited right of editorial control.'[9]

These brave words by Lord Normanbrook did not alter the fact that while Sir Hugh Greene was Director-General, he encountered very little effective opposition from the governors. Nearly all of them would have supported him when he said in Rome in February 1965: ' In its search for truth, indeed in whatever it undertakes, a broadcasting organization must recognize an obligation towards tolerance and towards the maximum liberty of expression . . . I believe that broadcasters have a duty not to be diverted by arguments in favour of what is, in fact, disguised censorship. I believe we have a duty to take account of the changes in society, to be ahead of public opinion rather than always to wait upon it . . . Relevance is the key – relevance to the audience and to the tide of opinion in society. Outrage is impermissible. Shock is not always so. Provocation may be healthy and indeed socially imperative.'[10]

Greene saw the BBC as in the mainstream of a cultural flow. He now had to work with a man like Lord Hill, all of whose recent experience was gained with the ITA. Hill did not see the ITA as a creative catalyst, although it was involved with creative decisions. Instead, in a speech in May 1964 in London, he stated: 'In the nature of its responsibilities the Authority has to function to some degree as a censor. The two Acts say that television must do nothing that offends against good taste or decency. Nothing must be seen that is offensive to public feeling. Contentious issues must be presented with complete impartiality

. . . Well, we have a very simple yardstick, the yardstick of commonsense. Some people decry commonsense. They say that it's muffling and stifling. But I don't agree. At any rate, a bit of commonsense, intelligently applied, never did much harm. A line has to be drawn. Very well, then let us all agree not to strike fundamental attitudes for or against censorship, but simply try to draw the line in a sensible human way, and may I say, without losing our sense of humour.'[11]

Sir Hugh Greene and Lord Hill clearly differed in their approach to the role and functions of broadcasting in the sixties. Those around them feared a terrible clash. The acting Chairman, Robert Lusty, a great friend of the Director-General, told Lord Hill that the BBC governors were shocked at the news of his appointment; that he foresaw great difficulties ahead, and he offered to mediate between Hill and Greene. But Hill was not to be muzzled so easily. He soon concluded that the governors decided very little and that 'a common form of so-called decision was what the governors agreed with the Director-General'. He found that the governors' discussions, 'however exciting, however valuable, seemed to lead nowhere. A point was made, the Director-General replied, and that was that.' [12] Clearly this was not a state of affairs that Hill found acceptable.

The early months brought renewed public controversy for the BBC, this time mainly in the area of current affairs. Certain governors echoed letters from the public when they said that the underlying purpose of 24 Hours seemed to be to 'discover anything that was good or anything that had existed for some time and then seek to destroy it'. Those writing to the BBC expressed concern about the negative spirit they felt was in evidence. Why was everything knocked? There seemed to be little control over the producers by anyone.

Faced by these not unfamiliar criticisms Lord Hill agreed that a paper should be drawn up setting out what should be the relationship between the mood of the country and the BBC. In Greene's absence at the Commonwealth Broadcasting Conference, Oliver Whitley prepared the first draft, and Lord Hill revised it. 'Broadcasting and the Public Mood'[13] did not quite hit the target it was intended to hit! Coming from the Board of Governors, it was unlikely to appeal to rank and file producers with their suspicions that they were being asked to 'trim' their programmes in order to avoid controversy.

Lord Hill was able to strengthen his control inside the BBC because of a spate of new appointments that had to be made by the governors. The most important of the new appointments was that of Director-General. Sir Hugh Greene asked to go. The fact that his wife was divorcing him was not the reason for his departure, but it did affect the timing of the announcement of his departure. Greene and Hill discussed the matter in May 1968. In July it was announced that he would retire as Director-General in April 1969, and become a governor in July 1969, the first Director-General ever to do so. The announcement of Greene's departure delighted Mrs Whitehouse. T. C. Worsley in the *Financial Times* put it well when he wrote that Greene 'carried the BBC struggling and kicking out of its auntie image into something more relevant to the decade. Instead of reflecting the respectable old-fashioned middle-class values of the past that were over and done with, the BBC began to mirror at least equally the aspirations and attitudes of the newly enfranchised young who had come up via the grammar schools and the red-brick universities . . . Sir Hugh gave them their chance.'

Frank Gillard, Director of Radio, and Kenneth Adam, Director of Television, both retired at the end of 1969. So management re-organization began. Five candidates were interviewed by the Board of Governors for the post of the Director-General: Charles Curran, Oliver Whitley, Kenneth Lamb, Huw Wheldon, and David Attenborough. Curran was unanimously appointed, with Huw Wheldon becoming Managing Director of television and David Attenborough his number two. Ian Trethowan was chosen as Managing Director of radio, a welcome choice of someone outside the BBC's top echelons. He possessed a wealth of practical experience in television reporting that helped radio to update its approach to current affairs broadcasting.

Lord Hill's strategy had been helped in 1968 with the appointment of three new governors – Robert Bellinger, Tom Jackson of the Post Office workers union and Dame Mary Green. All three supported Lord Hill loyally. All three were determined to be active governors, not ciphers. Not long after, a small incident proved that changes were in the wind. Lady Baird, one of the governors, who was also a doctor, felt that the *Radio Times* should cease to accept cigarette advertisements, even though the decision would mean the loss of a quarter of a million pounds a year. Despite the Board of Management's express wish to continue the governors ruled against the practice by a majority of five to four. The senior staff, including Greene, Lamb, Whitley and Curran, were all appalled at the way their desire to continue these advertisements was rejected by the Board. But Lord Hill refused to give way. The job of the governors was to govern, preferably in agreement with the Board of Management, but if agreement was not possible, the governors' views were to prevail.

The BBC power game

Lord Hill's move towards building the Board into an effective executive was to tackle both the question of the BBC's finance and the introduction of effective sub-committees of the Board of Governors in a single move. Right at the beginning of his chairmanship, when Harold Wilson asked Hill to make a personal study of the BBC's finances, he had requested a special investigation of possible economies and alternative ways of raising money.

Successive governments had tended to postpone increases in the licence fee because of electoral considerations.

But the BBC governors were themselves partly to blame for the fact that government gave the BBC a low financial priority. Lacking specialized knowledge of the Corporation's finances, they dealt with spending proposals quite superficially and speedily. Hill decided that three members of the Board should constitute a finance committee 'which would scrutinize financial proposals with considerable care before they came to the board, and maintain a continuous watch on spending generally'. Three other members of the Board, Dame Anne Godwin, Lady Baird and Glanmor Williams, all of whom had longer experience as governors than Lord Hill, opposed this suggestion, since they saw it as constricting the Corporation's 'clever and dedicated top officials'. Hill put it to the vote, which carried his proposal by five to three. Now Hill had placed responsibility for finance firmly back under the Board's corporate decision-making process, but with far more information at its disposal, not only from its own sub-committee, but also with the advantage of information gathered by McKinseys, the outside firm of management consultants.

When McKinseys delivered their report in 1968, they proposed wide changes in management structure. Their leader, Roger Morrison, stated bluntly that the purpose of their recommendations was 'to build into the BBC a positive system of management which did not depend on the spending of money handed down from above but which would demand the active participation of those spending the money, in the setting and achieving of objectives related to the more effective and economic use of available resources'.[14] A wide range of proposals included the establishment of productivity targets, the strengthening of planning and control of information, and the streamlining of administrative procedures. Greene accepted all the proposals except one that dealt with the managerial control over news. The whole exercise was a clear illustration of the new-found powers of the Board of Governors to alter the internal structures and organization of the BBC, albeit indirectly.

By 1972 alterations in the control of news were attempted too. Hill explained his thinking to the other governors in a paper which included the following passage: 'The question I have been turning over in my mind for some time is whether by organizational changes there could be brought

more coherence, more top level co-ordination and super-
vision to a crucial branch of broadcasting which from now
on is likely to be a source of attack on the BBC in a world
in which conflict abounds and in which Parliament appears
resentful of a medium which it believes, rightly or wrongly,
to be more powerful than itself.' But throughout his chairmanship Hill found that, try as he did, with plentiful
assistance from the Board of Management, the politicians
of both parties were constantly complaining about and
attempting to influence BBC coverage.

By 1972 Lord Hill had finally achieved his object: a
very different Board of Governors with a far more positive
approach to its duties was in control. Hill wrote in his
diary on 1 June 1972: 'Only in the last six months have
the governors, by their composition and their attitude,
begun really to assume their proper responsibilities particularly as trustees for the public. Recent appointments
have made all the difference, as has the disappearance of
the last traces of adherents of the Greene view that the
governors were there mainly to support what the executive
did or wanted to do.' Hill had tamed the BBC Board of
Management. But with the politicians who appointed him
he had not been so successful.

The BBC versus Labour politicians

The departure of Sir Hugh Greene had partly mollified the
moral protesters. Lapses of taste continued to occur from
time to time, but the NVALA now felt they had a friend at
court. Whereas under Greene the BBC came under
strongest attack for its drama, with sex, language and violence as the favourite targets, and a Viewers' Council as the
recommended remedy, the new target now became news
and current affairs, and the main complaints from the politicians. A general election which Labour – though firm
favourites – lost, and increasing troubles in Ulster, made
the BBC's job of presenting the facts as it saw them even
more difficult.

Harold Wilson had not been overfond of the BBC since
the heady days of the run-up to the Labour victory in 1964.

By 1966 he had become sufficiently disenchanted deliberately to snub John Morgan, who hoped to interview him on the train returning from Huyton on the first day of his election victory. After various other disagreements, his appointment of Lord Hill was seen in some quarters as some sort of revenge for the way he had been treated earlier. But if Lord Hill was expected to 'control' the BBC, then clearly those who hoped he would were disappointed.

Harold Wilson regularly complained of his treatment at the hands of the BBC both as Prime Minister and as Leader of the Opposition. The first of many clashes came in April 1968 when a comedian used of the Prime Minister the phrase once used of Lyndon Johnson – 'If his lips move he's lying'. The BBC apologized. Hill visited Wilson at the House of Commons, and was treated to a long recital of the Corporation's wickedness going back over many years. Hill wrote later, 'clearly he disliked the BBC; I do not doubt that his belief that the BBC was continuously unfair was genuine'. In order to improve the BBC's relationships with Westminster after this event the Secretary of the Corporation, Kenneth Lamb, was detailed to spend half his time on making better contacts with Westminster and Whitehall. But attacks on the Prime Minister on *Any Questions*, *The World this Weekend* and even the music programme *Night Ride* continued.

Rows continued during 1969. In December Lord Hill was summoned to Number 10. 'Twice in five weeks, Harold Wilson said, the Prime Minister had been refused an opportunity to come to the screen, once on the fifth anniversary of his government taking up office and now in *Panorama*. Any pretence that we could not put him on during the debate was destroyed by the fact that we had put on others. This had led him to rethink his whole relationship to the BBC.'[15]

1970 was an election year. Both broadcasting organizations braced themselves for the inevitable charges of bias. For too many politicians a programme is impartial if it leans to their direction, and hostile if it does not. Wilson liked to suggest which of his ministers should cover various

topics. For the election *Panorama* on foreign affairs he suggested Denis Healey rather than the Foreign Secretary, Michael Stewart, saying that he thought defence should be the topic. Sir Alec Douglas-Home was to appear for the Tories – but declined to appear in debate with Denis Healey. The upshot was that both did separate pieces from different parts of the country.

At his press conference the following morning Wilson claimed that it was for the parties to nominate speakers and subjects. In reply the BBC issued the following statement: 'The BBC wishes to make it clear that, party political and party election broadcasts apart, the parties do not nominate speakers or choose issues in BBC political programmes. The BBC takes the initiative, and in the case of the election editions of *Panorama* offers the parties the opportunity to comment on the major issues selected and consults the parties on speakers before inviting them to take part.' Angry exchanges between the Prime Minister and the Director-General continued right up to nine o'clock on election night about the respective amounts of time devoted to Heath and Wilson. The final conversation ended with Wilson hinting darkly that he would deal with the BBC after the election. But in the outcome the Conservatives won. This type of skirmishing continued under the 1974 Labour Government, with an especially passionate denunciation of the BBC's unfairness to Labour during the October 1974 election being made by Ron Hayward after the results were announced.

Under the new Conservative administration two major confrontations were to occur. First the *Yesterday's Men* incident with the Labour party, then the *Question of Ulster* programme which angered so many Conservatives. The *Yesterday's Men* saga began when David Dimbleby wrote to Harold Wilson and other former Labour cabinet ministers asking them to take part in a programme about the political and personal nature of the job of Opposition. Mr Wilson agreed to take part. Later Dimbleby wrote to say that he and the producer Miss Angela Pope had decided the film 'will be about the defeat and its impact in political and personal terms and about the problems Opposition poses'. Finally they both went to see him and explained that they intended to make a responsible and serious programme in which they would wish to interpolate some personal details in so far as these were relevant. What they did not say was what the programme was to be called and that a pop group called 'The Scaffold' would be adding musical numbers entitled 'Humpty Dumpty' and 'Yesterday's Men'. Early in May the interview took place at the Lime Grove studios, and according to the BBC tape the following exchange took place:

DIMBLEBY: Many of your colleagues have told us that they are suffering financially from being in opposition, but you are said to have earned something between £100,000 and £250,000 from writing this book. Has that been a consolation to you over this time?

WILSON: I would not believe any of the stories you read in the press about that. My press handling for a long period of time has been one of rumour. If they got the facts, they twisted them. Anything personal – if they did not get the facts, they invented them. So you can dismiss that from the case right away. I think I got fair compensation for what I wrote, but I would not accept any of those views. I get a salary as Leader of the Opposition.

DIMBLEBY: You could not set our minds at rest on the vexed question of what the *Sunday Times* actually did pay you for it?

WILSON: No. I do not think it is a matter of interest to the BBC or anybody else. If you are interested in these things, you had better find out how people buy yachts. Did you ask that question? Did you ask him how he was able to pay for a yacht? Have you asked him that question?

DIMBLEBY: I have not interviewed him.

WILSON: Well, has the BBC ever asked that question?

DIMBLEBY: I do not know.

WILSON: What has it got to do with you then?

DIMBLEBY: I imagine –

WILSON: Why do you ask this question – if people can afford to buy £25,000 yachts? Did the BBC not regard that as a matter for public interest? Why do you come snooping with these questions?

DIMBLEBY: It is only that it has been a matter of speculation –

WILSON: All I am saying –

DIMBLEBY: . . . and I am giving you an opportunity, if you want it, to say something about it.

WILSON: It was not a matter of speculation. You are just repeating press gossip. You have not put this question to Mr Heath. When you have got an answer from him, come and put that question to me. This last question and answer are not to be recorded.

DIMBLEBY: By any standards –

WILSON: Is this question being recorded?

DIMBLEBY: Well, it is, because we are running the film.

WILSON: Well, will you cut it out or not? All right, we will stop now. No, I am sorry. I am really not having this.

ANGELA POPE (Producer): Yes, of course we will.

Further argument took place, during which Wilson said, 'I do not want to read in "Miscellany" (in *The Guardian*) or *The Times* "Diary" that I asked for it to be cut out,' and again, 'if this film is used or if this is leaked, then there is going to be a hell of a row.' On 10 June the London *Evening Standard* printed a version of the story, which was taken up by all the national press the next day.

Yesterday's Men was scheduled to be transmitted on 17 June. As late as the evening before the BBC was confused as to whether it should comply with Mr Wilson's request or not. Wilson's Press Secretary, Joe Haines, was certain that John Crawley, BBC Editor of News and Current

Affairs, had agreed with him that all questions and answers would be omitted. John Crawley believed that his assurance related only to the third question. Sir Charles Curran, the Director-General, was prepared to accept the Haines version until the evening of the 16th, when after a talk with Huw Wheldon, Managing Director of Television, and Desmond Taylor, he changed his mind. The issue was settled the following morning by the Board of Governors who previewed the programme themselves, and decided to remove all three questions. Though Sir Hugh Greene, at that time a governor, dissented, Lord Hill decided that 'in the circumstances of the confusion about the character of the undertaking, we were bound to honour it as Haines had interpreted it, as covering the three questions'.[16] Wilson's legal adviser Lord Goodman had also asked that photographs of Wilson's houses should be removed on grounds of security, and that the name of the programme was misleading and should be changed. These further requests were refused.

When the programme was shown, the press comment was generally hostile to the BBC. The *Sun* said that by omitting the three questions, the BBC had caved in to Wilson. *The Times* said the programme was 'too shallow to be tolerated', and *The Guardian* that the producer, Angela Pope, had produced 'a giggly, gossipy documentary full of snide visuals and engagingly crass questions of the "would-you-stab-Harold-in-the-back" variety.' This was for me an apt description of the sort of programme that Ned Sherrin, producer of *TW3*, does far better. The important difference is that Ned Sherrin makes entertainment programmes, while Miss Pope was attempting a programme 'about the problems Opposition poses'. Later in the week the *New Statesman* accused the BBC of releasing a programme grotesquely different from the one in which the former Ministers had agreed to participate. It condemned 'this licence to distort and misrepresent which the BBC concedes to its producers'. Lord Goodman added fuel to the fire by announcing that Wilson was considering a libel action which would concentrate on David Dimbleby's reference to his 'privileged access' to government papers.

Lord Hill intervened again, this time by setting up an internal enquiry. Some governors wanted a 'severe condemnation of those who had made the programme'; the actual report did nothing of the kind. It stated that the questions about Mr Wilson's earnings were perfectly permissible, and were only omitted because of confusion as to the exact nature of undertakings given to Mr Haines. Furthermore the material selected for use in the transmitted programme had been fair, with no improper intercutting. Against this, the participants should have been told the title and they should have known of the theme music and the illustrations, because these coloured the presentation; part of the programme was too frivolous in comparison with the main content. The Board's report was drawn up by men and women who failed to understand some of the problems of current affairs broadcasting. The special investigator appointed, Maurice Tinniswood, was in fact in charge of personnel. Those inside the Current Affairs Group did not feel particularly proud of the programme. It clearly needed more shape.

I have recounted the whole incident at length, despite the fact that similar if less celebrated events have occurred before and since, because this one led to detailed involvement by the governors in a way that would have been unthinkable earlier. Lord Hill's action had been to assert powers, long held by the governors, which had lain dormant since the Beveridge Committee *Report* of 1949. The governors' function was to resemble that of a Minister of State: 'The governors who constitutionally form the Corporation, must assume and must have power to perform effectively the function of a Minister in keeping his department in touch with public opinion and subject to external criticism. The channel for informed democratic control of broadcasting must lie in the governors. The governors should have tenure and pay related to this as their essential function. The charter should place them in unfettered control of the staff and all its activities, for only if they have full authority can they feel fully responsible. The charter should require them to have organs for receiving and considering public opinion.' [17]

Lord Normanbrook had taken this doctrine to heart; his comprehensive lecture stated that 'within the BBC, the ultimate level of decision, even executive decision on matters of importance, lies in the Board of Governors, or, in a matter of urgency, the Chairman acting under the authority delegated to him by the Board'.[18] Lord Normanbrook found however that his fellow governors were not behind him in this interpretation of a more 'interventionist' role for the Board. Lord Hill found the same situation. He wrote, 'In my first two years there was but marginal strengthening of the role of governors, because only a minority wanted it. Only when the composition of the board changed was substantial progress really possible.' [19]

When Lord Hill retired he was reasonably happy that the Board's position was at last comparable with that of a Minister dealing with his Permanent Secretary. The Board decided the larger questions of policy and finance, together with management questions if the Director-General asked them. The Board made the senior appointments, and was responsible for the major exchanges between the BBC and outside bodies. 'It should not intervene in the programme-making process or, save in exceptional circumstances, see or hear programmes before transmission. It should be informed of major changes in programme policy and of developments in public and political opinion, and should listen to the advisory bodies. Before reaching its decisions, the board should consult the Director-General and senior colleagues; once made, responsibility for implementation of these decisions rests with the Director-General.'

Sir Hugh Greene and many of the earlier boards of management would unquestionably consider that these tenets represented an improper invasion of the scope of the Director-General. However, vast areas of programme decisions and management control remain in the Director-General's power. The difference today is that if the governors dislike the results of his policies, they will not remain silent. Tom Jackson, in his final year as governor, felt the changes had not gone far enough. He felt the Board was like the organizer of a bus trip who staffed the bus and filled it with petrol, but had no control over its destination. Like other governors, Jackson wanted a greater knowledge of programme plans in advance. In that he may have been wrong, but anyone who has read the *Beveridge Report* knows the governors are not yet fully channels of democratic control.

The birth of the Programme Complaints Commission

The *Yesterday's Men* affair left commentators divided. Some felt the BBC had caved in to pressure from Harold Wilson; others that the whole programme had been a mistake. Bob Mellish, then Labour Chief Whip, said there was 'a limit to how much a democracy can abuse, insult, sneer and jeer'. The BBC published its report on the events which included the following; to many it amounted to no more than a grudging apology. 'Politics is a minefield. There is inevitably a divergence between the aims of politicians and the aims of journalists, whether of the press or of broadcasting. The politician may want to expose his views of the truth, whereas the journalist wants to expose all the truth as he knows it. Nevertheless, each needs the other, and ground rules have been developed on which trust and understanding rest. This incident has impaired that relationship, and the BBC greatly regrets that this should be so. It will play its part in restoring understanding. We shall, however, do nothing that could put at risk the independence of the BBC. Broadcast journalism has special obligations, but it cannot surrender to any individual or party or government – any more than can the press – its right of independent editorial judgment.'

The report had a mixed reception in the press. Headlines included 'BBC rejects charges' and 'BBC Refuses to Apologize Over Controversial Yesterday's Men'. *The Guardian* attacked both sides but concluded that 'the BBC will have to be more sensitive next time'. The *Daily Ex-*

press said that the governors were right to take the public interest as their guiding principle. In contrast the *Daily Telegraph* thought that the BBC sometimes forgot their duty to place fairness and objectivity before sheer entertainment value. To the BBC hierarchy the most alarming of all criticisms was that in the *Daily Mirror*, which called for 'an effective and accessible watchdog like the Press Council'.

Clearly the public would not easily accept that the governors could be wholly impartial in matters affecting programmes for which they were required to take the ultimate responsibility. Individuals might feel they had been unjustly treated in many ways which broadcasters would regard as normal practice. Complaints often allege unfair editing and juxtapositions, inadequate reporting, unfair questioning, reconstruction of incidents and misconduct by staff. Although all these practices were against BBC codes of practice, clearly some people thought that abuses did occur.[20]

The idea of a Broadcasting Council had been put forward before the *Yesterday's Men* affair by Julian Critchley, and published by the Conservative Political Centre (CPC) in January 1971.[21] Critchley wanted a body like the Press Council with a retired Lord of Appeal as its chairman. Unlike the Press Council, it would not be a voluntary body, and members of the public would be predominant, holding seven of the twelve places. These seven would include politicians, newspaper-journalists and one representative from the viewers' associations. Its findings would be carried by the channel concerned, and published by the *Radio Times* and *TV Times*. The Broadcasting Council would reinforce, but in no way supersede, the powers of the 'supervisory' bodies which already exist. Critchley did not think that the Broadcasting Council would be a simple solution to all the failings of television, and he was certain that the broadcasting organizations would not take up the idea unless the Minister, at that time Christopher Chataway, prompted them. In fact, Chataway at first liked the scheme, then privately rejected it. Mr Heath also liked the idea, and asked Brian Forbes the film maker to draft some possible terms of reference for such a council.

Hill had first put the idea of his Complaints Commission to the governors at the same time as the CPC published Critchley's plans. Matters drifted and in July the Director-General, Sir Charles Curran, came back with proposals for an ombudsman. Sir Hugh Greene, who was absent, wrote opposing it. Then sensing the possibility of moves by the government, Hill moved fast, deciding to have an ombudsman committee of three. By the end of the month he had approached the ex-ombudsman Sir Edmund Compton, the ex-Speaker of the House of Commons, Horace King, and the ex-Lord Chief Justice, Lord Parker. In their haste both Hill and Curran forgot to tell the BBC General Advisory Council, who were rightly annoyed. A special meeting should have been called in the light of so important a development. Chataway seemed less than delighted – perhaps there was to have been an announcement of a Broadcasting Council at the forthcoming Conservative Party Conference. Hill wrote in his diary for October, 'They regard us as having killed or at least injured their fox.'

The Programme Complaints Commission was described by *The Times* as being a 'modest concession' and by the *Daily Telegraph* as unlikely to satisfy those who wanted a Broadcasting Council. The rules limit what a complainant can do. He must raise a complaint to the BBC in writing within 30 days, and then if dissatisfied with their explanation raise the matter with the Commission within the next 30 days. He also has to undertake in writing not to go to the courts. The BBC agrees to publish the adjudication result, is free to comment on the verdict, and to decide what subsequent action, if any, is called for. Complaints are to be heard in private, and complainants must bear their own costs. Finally the Commission does not cover questions of taste. It could be said that the public had been promised some heavy artillery, and had in fact been provided with a pea-shooter.

Sir Hugh Greene resigned his governorship, then wrote to *The Times* complaining about this 'short-sighted attempt at appeasement', which he went on to state was 'the deplorable surrender by the present Board of Governors of responsibility and authority'. Hill was stung to reply on the day the letter was published – his words neatly sum up the situation that exists to the time of writing in 1976: 'Was there, we asked ourselves, something in the argument that the BBC is both the judge and the defendant? Is justice always seen to be done? The commission is not a broadcasting council: it is a move in the direction of being fair. But the setting-up of our commission is being used by the advocates of a broadcasting council to reactivate the arguments for controlling the broadcasters. Control. Censorship. Suppression. However the words are packaged in the clamour for a broadcasting council, those are the ones built into the argument . . . It is fallacious and dangerous to pretend that the errors inherent in freedom can be prevented by an external regulatory or controlling body with no responsibility for the creative process.'

For the BBC, then, rules of conduct which bind producers, plus the principle of 'upwards referral' of difficult points form the 'system of responsibility' that it operates in place of any overt censorship by the governors or management. But it is a delicate position, constantly under attack both internally and externally.

The IBA and programme content: the McWhirter affair

The IBA decided neither to participate in the BBC's Complaints Commission, nor to set up a commission of its own. Instead a small staff at the IBA was created to undertake the task of enquiring into complaints arising from programmes made by the independent companies.

Among various celebrated incidents that occurred was the attempt by Mr Norris McWhirter to ask the High Court to grant him an injunction stopping the IBA from transmitting a film made by ATV about Andy Warhol. His grounds were that the IBA had failed to observe provision 1(a) of the Television Act which states that 'nothing shall be included in the programmes which offends against good taste or decency or is likely to be offensive to public feeling'. McWhirter claimed that he had a sufficient interest as the owner of a television set who had paid his licence fee to seek the Court's injunction. He felt he was entitled to expect that programmes would comply with the Television Act.

At the time of his application the governors of the IBA had not seen the programme, and his injunction was granted. By the time the case was heard both the members of the Authority and the IBA general advisory council had seen it. Both bodies overwhelmingly deemed the programme suitable for transmission. Once the IBA had decided this, the court had no right to interfere. The judge however gave his own opinions when he concluded, 'The Authority should always remember that there was a silent majority of good people who said little but viewed a lot. Their feelings were to be respected as well as those of the vociferous minority who, in the name of freedom, shouted for ugliness in all its forms. So let the programme be shown. The court would not stop it.' [22]

Compared with the BBC, the IBA has run into comparatively little trouble. It has been careful to observe sensitive areas of taste, and has not angered the politicians of either

DAILY EXPRESS   JANUARY 16, 1973

"I hope you put the children to bed before that Warhol sex film came on."

party in the same way as the BBC. Perhaps the nature of ITN is more factual, less investigative, than its BBC equivalent. Thames, Granada, Yorkshire and London Weekend have current affairs departments, but all four together hardly add up to the size of BBC Current Affairs. Never the front-leader in daring, the ITA and its successor the IBA have escaped the attacks levelled at the BBC.

The BBC and Conservative politicians

If 1971 was the year of the big dispute between the Labour party and the BBC, then in 1972 the Conservatives had their turn. There had already been frictions in 1970–71 over the introduction of commercial radio, with Chataway abandoning his more extreme position after representations from the BBC. But all this was as nothing to the storm of anger that broke out when the BBC announced plans for a programme entitled *A Question of Ulster*. The idea was for a long and thorough programme that would look below the surface of violence and coolly examine solutions being offered. The intention was to look to the future, and not let participants apportion blame for the past. The programme would be live, under a neutral and judicial president leading a three-man 'tribunal', with the idea of copying the United States Senate Committee hearings. The use of the word 'tribunal' was one the BBC was later to regret, because some alleged that the programme infringed the government's sphere by trying to set itself up in judgement on solutions to Ulster's problems.

The Home Secretary, Reginald Maudling, who had specific responsibility for Northern Ireland, demanded to see the Chairman Lord Hill and the Director-General and told them he had serious doubts about the wisdom of the idea. He believed it had a built-in bias, because only one speaker in the main part of the programme would represent the Ulster Unionists, with seven expressing various dissenting views. Only one of the speakers favoured internment. Hill replied that the programme was a genuine attempt to present a fair picture from a variety of angles, that such a programme would be valuable, and that he could not agree to abandon it.

Following this meeting at the Home Office, the Conservative Government set out to use every method available to them, short of banning the programme outright, to make sure it did not appear. Newspaper stories appeared saying that the programme had been abandoned. The Stormont Government announced that it would not allow any representative to take part. The *Daily Telegraph* began a campaign against what it alleged to be the BBC's irresponsibility in its willingness to be used as a propaganda vehicle for those who advocated violence.

In reply to this the BBC issued a statement which began: 'The BBC believes such a programme to be in the public interest and that the suppression of views, however unpopular, would be both unwise and dangerous . . . If, however, it be true that the Stormont Government is now unwilling to co-operate, then the programme cannot proceed in the form planned for January 5th, and fresh thought will have to be given to its preparation for a later showing. The BBC recognizes the formidable difficulties of producing such a programme, but is confident of its ability to do so. What the BBC cannot accept is that it should be diverted from its public purpose of presenting all points of view by a campaign of pressure by a newspaper or anyone else.'

The Times backed the BBC by saying 'the programme should be shown' and so did *The Guardian*. The *Daily Telegraph* continued its opposition, and the *Sun* said, 'Stop this Mock Trial'. The problem of no Unionist MP appearing on the programme was solved by the intervention of Jack Maginnis, a Unionist MP who believed the Unionist case should be heard, and was willing to put it.

On the day before the programme the Home Secretary took the unusual step of sending Hill a letter by hand in which he stated that the programme 'in the form in which it had been devised could do no good and could do serious harm'. Hill immediately replied, 'If we shared your views that such a programme would worsen the situation in

Ulster we would not dream of proceeding with it. On the contrary we hope and believe that it will be of value in widening understanding of the issues involved.' When the programme began it had seven and a half million viewers, and over half that audience remained until it ended after midnight. Whereas before the programme telephone calls to the BBC were 10:1 against, after it they were 5:1 in favour. Though the press remained divided, *The Times* concluded that 'those who watched the programme from start to finish must have emerged with a deeper understanding of the complexities of the Northern Irish situation.'

Hill's diary recorded the comment, 'One cannot help reflecting that when I was appointed here the accusation was that I was a government stooge put in to quell the BBC and keep it under control. In the event we had a bloody row last year with the Labour Party over *Yesterday's Men* and now a bloodier row with a Conservative government over this programme. The sweets of responsibility are delightful, but not all.'

A Question of Ulster was perhaps the BBC's great victory over hidden demands for censorship. However, many journalists believe that there has been an increasing degree of 'patriotic censorship' during the Northern Ireland troubles. The Conservative backbenchers pressed Reginald Maudling before *A Question of Ulster* to impose restrictions. Hill and Maudling met and the BBC subsequently issued a statement which concluded, 'as between the government and opposition, as between the two communities in Northern Ireland, the BBC has a duty to be impartial no less than in the rest of the United Kingdom. But as between the British Army and the gunmen the BBC is not and cannot be impartial.' This intensified the rumblings in the National Union of Journalists' radio and television shop, which declared in a resolution that 'We deplore the intensifying censorship in the television, radio and press coverage of events in Ireland and we pledge ourselves to oppose it'.

One day it will be possible to make more accurate statements about the extent of such censorship – how, where and by whom such controls were imposed. One day historians may be allowed to know the truth about a situation which is alleged to exist, but on which no more than hearsay evidence is adduced.

For commentators like Anthony Smith, the Whitley document was a kind of *Magna Carta*.[23] This is no doubt why he sees Lord Hill as a kind of 'bad King John', because while Hill and his like-minded governors did indeed 'with the Director-General discuss and then decide upon major matters of policy and finance', they did not really find themselves able to 'leave the execution of that policy and the general administration of the service in all its branches to the Director-General and his competent officers'. Anthony Smith sees the BBC governors before the advent of Lord Hill as 'a group of powerful people who were looking not to the immediate advantage of the BBC but to a set of national interests'. Under Sir Hugh Greene the powers of the Director-General as supreme in all aspects of the executive was maintained – until Lord Hill arrived in 1967. The governors now became more like BBC administrators than guardians of the national interest.

When we come to the *Yesterday's Men* incident we see not so much the weakness of the governors, but the unmasking of an inherently unsatisfactory position where the governors are seen to be judge, jury and investigators in a decision for which they had themselves ultimately been responsible because they had previewed the programme. But had they not also been, in the words of the Whitley document, acting as Trustees to safeguard the Broadcasting Service in the national interest? Would not previous governors have taken the same views as Hill, and indeed would not all previous Director-Generals save Sir Hugh Greene and Charles Curran also have taken the same view?

It is clear then that broadcasting autonomy is being challenged. The views of Sir Hugh Greene, and of former heads of current affairs departments like Grace Wyndham Goldie (who stated recently that the only people who know what the public like are the broadcasters) are now being challenged. The whole question of content and access has been a jealously guarded broadcaster's privilege. In our increasingly democratic age the old, platonic views of broadcasting by a self-appointed elite must give way to more general consensus views.

Fortunately there remains great freedom and little censorship – though some degree of internal guidance. But is it good enough? The question of access has been largely ducked. The right of reply by the public has been used by the broadcasters so ineptly as to drive responsible men like Professor Stuart Hood to demand despairingly a broadcasting council. The challenge of the seventies is to create new institutions in broadcasting to match the problems, the demands for participation and the opportunities provided by a developing technology. This challenge will not be met by wistful dreaming of those far-off days of *That Was The Week That Was*. 'Television is too important to be left to the broadcasters.' When Tony Benn first said that, he was greeted with howls of outrage by jealous professionals. But the implications of what he said are becoming more apparent.

Chapter Eleven

Purpose and Participation

Decisions taken during the five years 1975 to 1980 will set a pattern for broadcasting that will endure into the next century. Certainly the era ushered in by the Pilkington Committee has stretched into the seventies and that pattern will last until 1981, unless the Annan recommendations, when they come, are very rapidly implemented. So public discussion and debate about broadcasting is especially important now. First, let us look back.

Purpose and realization

The purpose of broadcasting as defined by the BBC and the ITA in 1960, differed. The BBC led by Sir Hugh Greene told the Pilkington Committee that they considered television to be one of the main factors influencing the values and moral attitudes of our society. The BBC's traditional policy had been 'to develop programmes over the widest possible range of content and treatment, while preserving a reasonable balance between programmes intended for relaxation and amusement and those of a more thoughtful kind'.[1] The Committee agreed that the BBC had done this, though they felt that 'the BBC had lowered their standards in some measure in order to compete with Independent television'. Their service had successfully realized the purposes of broadcasting. As a reward they were given a second channel – BBC 2.

The ITA, whose case was presented by Sir Ivone Kirkpatrick, did not accept the belief that television exerted a high degree of influence on society. As he described it, 'the responsibility of the broadcaster is primarily and necessarily passive'.[2] The Pilkington Committee condemned the

ITA because 'they do not sufficiently reckon with the effects of television on values and moral standards generally, and that this reveals itself in many of independent television's programmes of entertainment'. So the ITA did not get a second channel; instead the Pilkington recommendation was that the ITA should itself take over the advertising and programme-planning from the programme companies. The Conservatives then in power rejected this recommendation: but the idea still has merit.

Fifteen years later the position of the two rivals is very different. On the whole the strengthened ITA did a good job. The worst excesses of the quiz programmes were avoided and ITV programmes were no more and no less violent than those of the BBC. Gone are the enormous profits, whittled away by taxation through the television levy and by inflation. ITV programmes are sometimes superb, occasionally bad, often trivial, seldom shocking. In spite of representations they still have not been granted a second channel. Caught in a pincer grip between BBC 1 and BBC 2, their audience figures are losing their lead.

The BBC in 1976 is far bigger and broader than it was before Pilkington. But it lacks the support of some of its former friends, including that loosely termed group referred to as the 'Establishment', the Labour Party, the religious bodies and other worthies. The Greene regime, while it delighted the young, the bright and the radical, alienated part of this essential support, and though Lord Hill and Sir Charles Curran tried to recapture this through cautious policies, their success was limited. The BBC found itself increasingly short of money. Successive governments have been increasingly reluctant to raise the licence fee. BBC spokesmen talk much about money, less about purpose, and some would say that the differences between BBC 1 and ITV are increasingly hard to recognize. BBC programmes are sometimes superb, occasionally bad, too often trivial, sometimes shocking to the sensitive.

If the prime purpose of television is to provide entertainment programmes of an undemanding nature, informational programmes which support the *status quo*, and cultural programmes which patronize artist and audience alike, then both main channels would seem to be doing their job. But should not the purpose of a television service be to do more? Should it not realize that there are moral and cultural goals towards which every society must, however imperfectly, strive – and help in this struggle. Realizing this, should not television actively stimulate participation in our imperfectly democratic society?

Instead, broadcasting now increasingly stands on the sidelines of democratic and cultural advance. In spite of its many achievements, the ideal of a centrally-responsible public service on which British broadcasting was founded, has diminished. In part this is the result of growth. The founders of British broadcasting could not have foreseen the huge concentration of financial and institutional power that now characterizes both broadcasting institutions. Since Pilkington, the BBC has increasingly retreated from those ideals of public service to which it paid tribute. The pressures of ITV's commercial competition have increasingly diverted the energy of the BBC into defensive scheduling. Competition between BBC and ITV has been embittered by the rivalry of BBC programme-planners clashing with their former colleagues now working for ITV.

The challenge to the Annan Committee, and to the government which must implement its recommendations, is to decide whether the present diseases of British Broadcasting need medication or surgery. The pressures on the Committee will be those of conservatism, that seeks to adapt rather than to change. But palliatives may not suffice. Structural change may be essential if broadcasting institutions are going to evolve with the changing needs of society. There are two areas of possible sickness – in broadcasting content and broadcasting control.

Problems of content: violence

By the time an American child is fourteen, he will have seen 18,000 people killed on the screen. Richard Tobin in the American *Saturday Review* monitored eight hours of national and local television output in the United States.

He wrote, 'We marked down 93 specific incidents involving sadistic brutality, murder, cold-blooded killing, sexual cruelty and related sadism. Men (and even women and children) were shot by gunpowder, burned at the stake, tortured over live coals, trussed and beaten in relays, dropped into molten sugar, cut to ribbons (in colour), repeatedly kneed in the groin, beaten while being held defenceless by other hoodlums, forcibly drowned, whipped with leather belts . . .' At that period in 1967–68 eight out of ten programmes on the three major commercial networks NBC, CBS and ABC contained violence.

If the effect on socially inadequate adults of seeing continuously violent programmes is serious, what is the effect on immature and impressionable children? In Britain the amount of television violence is more strictly rationed than in America. The average British boy is likely to see about ten hours of television violence per week as against sixteen seen by an American boy. Leicester University's Television Research Committee has shown that both delinquent and non-delinquent boys show an overwhelming preference for violent programmes, given the choice.[3] Milton Shulman in his book *The Ravenous Eye* calculates that the average British boy spends one-seventh of his waking life in a violent environment, either seeing violence on television or at the cinema, or reading about it in comics, magazines and books. His figures can be challenged, but his main contentions about violence on the screen are hard to refute. These are fourfold: first, that 'violence is usually done by the good man for moral reasons . . . the best man is the man who is best at violence[4]'; second, that violence does not really hurt – horrible wounds are seldom shown; third, that there is little pity for the victims of violence – innocent and guilty alike they die because that's the way it is; and, fourth, that society demands little expiation for violence – good and bad alike use force and death to fulfil their purposes; violent law enforcers do not get punished.

Both in Britain and America the television industry goes to great lengths to discount the effects of television violence. The Television Research Committee wrote, 'It is interesting to note the reaction of the television industry to any research which purports to show that watching violence, or any other television experience, may have undesirable consequences for the viewer or society at large. One sometimes gets the impression that in the United States the media men have "experts" on hand whose main task is to counter the statements and look for the weaknesses in the work of any other "expert" whose work may be interpreted as an attack on television.'[5] Certainly the social scientists disagree as much among themselves as did the doctors who supported or denied the connection between smoking and lung cancer.

The two common defences against the charge that television violence has a damaging effect on children are either that television merely reinforces existing attitudes, or that screen violence has a valuable cathartic effect. Dr Hilde T. Himmelweit's famous research project between 1954 and 1956 is often used as a justification for these arguments. In fact she was by no means complacent about the effects of violence. She wrote, 'There is no need to prove that such programmes do harm . . . the strongest reason for criticizing them is their reiteration that life is cheap and that conflict can be solved by violence.'[6] In contrast, the British sociologist Dr Mark Abrams is essentially cautious: 'The abundance of this noxious material in the mass media is beyond dispute. But does it lead to direct imitative behaviour on the part of ordinary average children? The available evidence from research on these points among children is slight and often negative.'

The whole subject is fraught with conflicting opinions. However the findings of the American Commission on the Causes and Prevention of Violence surveyed all this evidence and came up with disturbing conclusions: 'The preponderance of the available research evidence strongly suggests that violence in television programmes can and does have adverse effects upon audiences – particularly child audiences . . . Television enters powerfully into the learning process of children and teaches them a set of moral and social values about violence which are inconsistent with the standards of a civilized society . . . Younger children and a large proportion of teenagers from low income families believe that people behave in the real world the way they do in the fictional world of television . . . We believe it is reasonable to conclude that a constant diet of violent behaviour on television has an adverse effect on human character and attitudes. Violence on television encourages forms of behaviour, and fosters moral and social values about violence in daily life which are unacceptable in a civilized society.'

Violence is not only fictional. Factual television contains plenty of pictures of violence. Most famous of all was the execution of the Nigerian soldier caught looting. This was so carefully staged for the television cameras that the order to fire was delayed while one cameraman reloaded his camera with film. In another example, American viewers were treated to a close-up of an American sergeant lopping off the ear of a dead Vietcong soldier as a trophy. Scenes like these on the screen cannot be excused just because they happened – but they are. They make 'good television'. When, during the most violent period of the Vietnam war, nightly bulletins were filled with pictures of legless men screaming with pain, the President of CBS news announced, 'I never ask myself whether my reporting provides a useful social service . . . there is nothing we wouldn't show apart from obscenity.'[7] Writing about the British scene, Ronald Butt said in the *Sunday Times*, 'We are used to burning monks and corpses over our coffee cups: the impact has a diminishing return and horror is transmuted into cow-like complacency.'

In defence of the service it offered, the BBC set up a special Research Advisory Group to assist in gauging the social effects of television, most specifically those connected with violence. This group first made a study in depth of the violence content in programmes and secondly a survey of the role played in viewers' lives by programmes containing violence. In the words of the report 'the findings of these surveys are largely unsensational'. But it added, 'the fact that many portrayals of violence on television have little significance for most of their viewers does not imply that such portrayals are harmless, whilst the variability of individual responses to violence serves as a reminder that all modes of presentation of aggression demand consideration.'[8]

Soon afterwards David Attenborough (then Director of Programmes, Television) issued a new set of notes for the guidance of producers and writers working in television. He stated that the basic aim of the producer in making his decisions on the portrayal of violence, in both fictional and documentary programmes, must be 'to sharpen and not to blunt the human sensitivities of the viewer . . . There may be occasions when the scenes of executions do help to make a genuine point which contributes to the viewer's understanding of events. Scenes of the execution of a looter in Nigeria were revealing a state of affairs in that country during the secession of Biafra and on those grounds could be justified. It should be kept in mind that violence seldom occurs without cause and that, whenever possible, the viewer is owed an explanation of the violence he is shown.'[9]

The ITV code on violence was also revised as a result of the growing imports of more violent programmes from America and elsewhere, and because of new research evidence. When issuing the new code the IBA. commented, 'Violence is not only physical: it can be verbal, psychological, and even metaphysical or supernatural. Whatever form the violence in a programme may take its inclusion can only be justified by the dramatic or informational context in which it is seen, and the skill, insight and sensitivity of the portrayal.'

Their document was for many wholly admirable. It considered the content of the programme schedule as a whole, stating that an acceptable minimum of violence in each individual programme may add up to an intolerable level over a period. It reiterated the ITV policy that 'family viewing time' until 9.00 p.m. entailed special concern for younger viewers. Speaking of the ends and the means, it stated that there is no evidence that the portrayal of violence for good or 'legitimate ends' is likely to be less harmful to the individual, or to society, than the portrayal of violence for evil ends. On presentation, the code also pointed out that it may be just as dangerous to society to conceal the results of violence or to minimize them, as to let people see clearly the full consequences of violent behaviour, however gruesome: but added that what may be better for society may be emotionally more upsetting or more offensive for the individual viewer. It concluded wisely with the injunction that ingenious and unfamiliar methods of inflicting pain or injury – particularly if capable of easy imitation – should not be shown without the most careful consideration.[10]

The violent content of programmes has raised continuous protest from a wide range of viewers since the late fifties. Both broadcasting organizations have codes of conduct which regulate violence on the screen. But the television producers both in factual and fictional programme-making have a problem. We live in a violent age. Any news cameraman covering a war is bound to film scenes of violence if he is up in the front line. No broadcasting organization would see its job as being to suppress the footage, even if it does omit some of the most gory scenes. Rather, its duty lies in seeking to explain the background situation which lies behind such violence. In fictional programmes our brightest young writers are interested to explore situations which are, for some, shocking. Not to allow such plays to be broadcast is to deny them and that part of the public at large which is not impressed by the arguments of the NVALA the opportunity for their work to be seen. Perhaps the expedient of warning audiences before the programme begins that a play may be shocking to some is the answer for the National Viewers' and Listeners' Association.

A Broadcasting Council?

There will never be unanimous agreement on questions of taste. Successive broadcasting inquiries have seen fit to refer all such questions to the broadcasting authorities themselves. Time and again questions of taste have been raised in Parliament, ranging from alleged obscenity in *That Was The Week That Was* to the political wisdom of allowing a programme like *A Question of Ulster* to be broadcast. Correctly, all Postmaster-Generals and their successors, the Ministers of Posts, have refused to comment on individual programmes. Sometimes the broadcasters have admitted their mistakes, sometimes they have denied that a mistake was made. The governors of the BBC and ITA are those entrusted by Parliament to represent the public. The advantage of the present system is that not only have the governors the power to investigate allegations of bad taste, but also the power to prevent similar incidents recurring. Such power is more theoretical than actual, because in the BBC questions are asked not before but after a programme is broadcast, and in the ITV companies only a small minority of programmes are seen by the IBA before transmission. Producers are given guidelines. In areas of doubt they are expected to refer decisions upwards.

A new factor in the representations of the NVALA and the moral and religious bodies is the demand for a broadcasting council which would act as an arbiter on a wide range of questions – including taste, fairness and the general output of both services. Though it is true that Mrs Whitehouse has been pressing for such a council for many years, the new interest of both political parties in such an idea makes it much more likely. As long ago as 1964 Mr Roy Mason MP said in a debate on broadcasting that 'many criticisms are being made of what is being broadcast but with no apparent satisfaction to the persons and organizations responsible for the criticisms. Therefore we think it is time that the Postmaster-General – not the BBC or the ITA – should set up a national advisory council to assist him in this work, a body representative of the radio and television industry, consumers, viewers, universities and possibly broadcasting personnel, with terms of reference wide enough for them to report on all matters affecting sound broadcasting and television, and more important, that they should be given authority to present to

Parliament an annual report which should be debated annually in the House.

'Parliamentary accountability over this range of broadcasting is badly lacking, and the adoption of this proposal would help to fill the gap. The House really needs some satisfaction on this score. Members have difficulty in raising points at Question Time and we have never debated the BBC and ITA Annual Reports. This idea of a general advisory council with teeth and with power could help the House and would make the sound and television authorities more accountable to Parliament.'

When Labour came to power, Roy Mason became Postmaster-General. He rapidly reconsidered his views and announced to the House: 'It would be wrong to establish additional machinery for the oversight of the conduct of the broadcasting services.' But the fire he had started was not so easily extinguished. If the governors of the broadcasting organizations and the advisory bodies really were functioning well, then there was no need for a further body which could only diminish their authority. But clearly there was a body of opinion that thought they were not beyond criticism.

The Scottish advisory body was often incensed at the way Scotland was treated. The Church Assembly was often dismayed by the approach adopted by the Central Religious Advisory Committee (CRAC). And those viewers or organizations who complained to either the BBC or ITA found little enough in the way of positive response apart from a polite non-committal letter. Far from representing the public, the governors displayed a determination to support the BBC as a first priority, with representations from the public being given a very secondary place. When, for example, the Bishop of Southwark not unreasonably criticized a facile *Panorama* item on the Church of England Lord Hill called the Bishop's criticism 'uncharitable, unfair and in important respects untrue'. It is regrettable that the Chairman of the Board should have had to question the integrity of a distinguished bishop in order to defend a rather slight piece by an agnostic producer.

The Programme Complaints Commission was introduced by the governors of the BBC because there was a fear within the BBC that the government might create some outside body along the lines of the broadcasting council suggested by Julian Critchley MP and others.[11] The Complaints Commission is a strange body. It is neither a creature of the BBC nor a fully independent arbitration commission. It is paid for by the BBC, which also drew up the rules. These include three clauses which a court of law might frown on. The first is that all complainants have to give their written undertaking that they will not make recourse to courts of law. (Some legal experts doubt whether such an undertaking could be upheld; it asks citizens to divest themselves voluntarily of one of their rights under British law.) The second is that all complaints have to be raised in writing with the BBC within thirty days of transmission, and then referred to the Complaints Commission within thirty days of the BBC's reply. The third clause is equally limiting. Complaints are heard in private and complainants must bear their own costs. Finally the BBC remains unbound by any action of the Complaints Commission. While it agrees to 'pay proper regard to the views expressed in each adjudication it shall be free to comment thereon and to decide what subsequent action, if any, is called for'.[12] This is a classic example of the 'heads we win, tails you lose' approach. By 1975 the Complaints Commission had heard only a handful of complaints, less than half of which were agreed by the Commission to be valid. Is it that the BBC is nearly perfect, or is it just a reflection of the Complaints Commission itself, owned and paid for as it is by the BBC?

The demand for a broadcasting council – some sort of public commission to which an aggrieved individual could apply in the event of misrepresentation or unfair treatment by a producer or broadcaster – was raised from time to time throughout the sixties. Instead of having to complain to the broadcasting authority itself, why should not the public be able to complain to a body like the Press Council, in which members of the public rather than broadcasters would be dominant? The Conservative Political Centre went as far as to publish Julian Critchley's eloquent little pamphlet in favour of a broadcasting council modelled somewhat on the lines of the Press Council, with non-broadcasters holding seven out of twelve places on the council, as well as the offices of chairman and vice-chairman. The non-broadcasters would include politicians, journalists and a representative from the viewers' associations. The findings of the council would not only be carried in the *Radio Times* and *TV Times*, but, more important, would be broadcast by the channels concerned.

Critchley concluded, 'I do not expect miracles, but the setting up of an impartial body for the investigation of grievances would be of some reassurance to the outraged, and would, over a period of time, build up a code of practice. Its sanctions would be indirect, but it is unlikely that a public corporation like the BBC would choose to ignore its findings, and the television companies, whose franchises are at risk, would take care not to offend.'[13]

More recently the Labour Party seems to have moved further in the direction of a broadcasting council with the publication of their discussion document *The People and the Media*. In it they put forward the idea of a communications commission. This body would have a permanent staff capable of initiating research into the long-term effects of television, and deciding on a range of technical matters including line standards. A secondary function would be for it to act as a complaints commission. The idea has yet to be worked out in detail, but in essence a body given the statutory responsibility by Parliament for planning the long-term developments in radio and television would be a formidable organization if it were also to handle day-to-day complaints.

Of course there is always the danger of broadcasters being stifled by too active a control on their freedoms. This risk has to be weighed against the charge that broadcasters are a fifth estate with more authority vested in them than was ever accorded to the fourth estate. Freedom to publish has modified press output in a way that freedom to broadcast cannot do, since there is no freedom to broadcast outside the narrow confines of two organizations that own a monopoly of the airwaves by virtue of their parliamentary licence.

The idea of a broadcasting council with wide powers has also been put forward by a very different body, namely the advertising industry, represented by the *Television 76* report produced jointly by the Incorporated Society of British Advertisers and the Institute of Practitioners in Advertising. They wrote, 'We propose that a Broadcasting Council be created which would assume powers and responsibility for regulating all sectors of radio and television broadcasting, whether commercial or non-commercial.'[14] The details we can leave to the next section of the chapter; the point here is that the powerful advertising lobby also sees a role for a broadcasting council.

Whether a broadcasting council would inspire a greater sense of purpose among broadcasters than the BBC and ITA are able to do is an interesting question. Undoubtedly the BBC inspires a tremendous loyalty and some magnificent work from many of its producers. But others are stifled by its sheer size, impersonality and bureaucracy. The independent companies do not suffer from the same problems of size, but some producers do suffer from insecurity, and a less clear sense of purpose, because they are perhaps mistakenly embarrassed by the fact that audience approval and advertising revenue are closely linked. In neither camp do programme-makers at any level have a real sense of participation in programme-planning – all that takes place at a far more exalted level. Democratic participation by the public in programme-making is not yet a live issue among broadcasters because, as with all professionals, ranks close when threatened by the intrusions of outsiders. *Open Door*, an access programme on BBC 1 in the late evenings was the brilliant idea of Rowan Ayres (formerly of BBC 2 *Late Night Line-Up*) which became the official BBC defence ploy to any further demands for access.

Plans for Reform

One of the last acts of the Wilson government in 1970 was to appoint Lord Annan as the chairman of a new Royal Commission on Broadcasting. At that time the charters of both the BBC and the IBA were due to expire in June 1976. A major reorganization seemed legislatively practical. But the incoming Conservative Government disbanded the Commission. It was determined to go ahead with its own plans for commercial radio without waiting for the deliberations of a Royal Commission. This did not prevent a wide range of other organizations from setting up their own independent committees during this period. As the political wheels of fortune turned full circle, the Annan Committee was reconvened by the new Labour Government in autumn 1974. Meanwhile the other committees had already reported on their own plans for reform. Among the many, we shall look briefly at just six of the most interesting.

One of the most radical plans was that just mentioned – from the advertising industry. Their plan proposed 'a reorganization which incorporated the best of both BBC and ITV'. They proposed that there should be four separate organizations. First was the Public Service Authority which would run two television channels out of the existing licence revenue, one a 'social and educational channel', the other a 'special interest' channel along the lines of BBC 2. The PSA would also run what is now BBC Radio. The next two separate organizations would be competing 'general interest' channels paid for out of advertising revenue, one owned by a public corporation like the BBC, the other by independent contractors like ITV, appointed by the Broadcasting Council. The same body would also run the fourth service – commercial radio. The ISBA/IPA report concluded rather smugly: 'These proposals will not only meet the needs of advertisers, but at the same time will satisfy the needs of all sectors of the community and will provide a wider choice than is at present available, at no extra cost to the public.'[15]

Meanwhile the IBA itself took soundings in the industry and came up with its own proposals for making the hitherto unallocated fourth channel into the exclusive preserve of the existing ITV companies. The second IBA channel was to complement the first, thus providing the opportunity for far more special-interest programmes, an opportunity largely denied to present ITV producers on the network basis. The idea of competing advertising channels put forward by the ISBA/IPA proposal was specifically rejected by the IBA. They commented, 'The fifteen different markets which ITV provides for advertisers represents the maximum competition which can exist without reducing programme standards and choices in a way that would be unacceptable.' [16] The Authority would act as a selector and co-ordinator of the dual ITV service by the simple expedient of taking two programme-planners on to the IBA staff. It was a neat idea, and for a few weeks it seemed if the Conservative Minister of Posts, Christopher Chataway, might have bought it. But press reaction was hostile, and Chataway tactfully drew back.

Within a year of making these proposals the IBA was under heavy fire itself from the Select Committee on Nationalized Industries.[17] This parliamentary committee attacked the IBA for excessive leniency in its policing duties, for favouring the larger companies, and for failing to ensure a broader range of programmes and more experimental approaches. It also took up the IBA's own idea of appointing two programme-planners to the IBA. The Committee's intelligent report found favour with the IBA, who agreed with most of the criticisms made while sticking to its claim for the fourth channel, and arguing that the present system of awarding contracts was the best that could be devised. While no reference was made to a broadcasting council, the Select Committee recommended to the Minister the need of a consumer organization for all communication media. Even the unions got a mention as having a right to discuss all questions of quality with the IBA.

Both the main broadcasting unions, the Association of Broadcasting Staff (mainly BBC) and the Association of

Cine and Television Technicians (mainly ITV and free-lance members) put in their own reports. ACTT was very concerned with unemployment among their members, and with the generally undemocratic nature of broadcasting control. The ABS had a highly original scheme of their own, first propounded by Anthony Smith in the pages of *The Guardian*. The idea was to form a National Television Foundation to run the fourth channel. The NTF was to be a charitable foundation taking money from the Television levy, the government and sponsors, and taking programmes from existing sources as repeats, from independent programme-makers, and from abroad. The NTF, without needing a huge bureaucracy, would be a publishing house opening its doors to all programme-makers, and to joint ventures with book publishers and even cassette publishers. Perhaps Anthony Smith was influenced by the vast sums pumped into programme-making from the BBC–*TimeLife* tie-up. How much more effective could a smaller, more flexible organization be.

The National Television Foundation plan was an attempt to devise a structure that would simply publish programmes. There were to be no studios, no staff producers, no institutionalized bureaucracy with its own exclusive loyalties and nepotism. Is it possible that, without its own accretions of practice, and house style, it might fail to build a regular audience? Planning the output of a television service demands skill, experience and some influence on the nature and consistency of the material to be broadcast. Programme-planners, like publishers, know the tastes of the audience for which they cater. Simply to push onto the air a totally unplanned sequence of programmes from diverse sources might only win a very small viewing audience. Plans for the NTF clearly need fuller research, but might be seriously considered by the Annan Committee.

Concern about the great size of the BBC and IBA complexes runs through many of the plans put forward. The NTF was an attempt to produce a new national channel which would be fed by far smaller units. Another communications expert, Professor Wedell, published an admirable plan to 'break down into sensible parts an organization which has become too big for its own, or the country's health'.[18] His plan was to have a series of broadcasting authorities each responsible for a channel, except for BBC 1 which would be a federation of regional broadcasting authorities, with full control over their own regional content. Local radio would have their own authorities, as would local cablevision channels if and when these emerge. National radio would have two authorities – one for Radio 1 and 2, another for Radio 3 and 4. The IBA is already a federal structure; losing control of commercial radio, it would continue to administer the present programme companies. Each broadcasting authority would operate under a licence from the Minister of Posts; finance would be provided by a National Broadcasting Finance Board.

In October 1972 came the verdict of the most distinguished broadcasting practitioner alive today. Sir Hugh Greene in a celebrated Granada *Guildhall Lecture*[19] gave his verdict on what should be done. First he wanted the BBC and ITA charters extended until July 1981. (The Conservative Government did just that.) Then he recommended that a major new enquiry should begin work in 1977. Its job would be to pay particular attention to the major technical developments that would have considerable effects on broadcasting after 1985. He recommended that the fourth channel should be given to the IBA on the basis first put forward by the Pilkington Committee – that is, the IBA itself would take over the functions of programme planning and selling advertising time. So in relation to ITV 2 the programme-contracting companies would simply have the function of producing programmes, not scheduling them. Nor was even this privilege solely theirs; a National Television Foundation would be established to encourage experimental work for ITV 2, and would be paid for programmes transmitted by the IBA. While the NTF would be guaranteed adequate daily airtime and hence daily income from the IBA it would be free to accept funding from other sources.

Sir Hugh Greene, now no longer an uncritical supporter

of the BBC, made other recommendations. The BBC and IBA should set up a joint executive committee to avoid undesirable programme clashes. Coverage of public events should alternate or be shared in the interests of the viewing public, as the present competitive coverage was wasteful. Shared audience research and a joint *Radio* and *TV Times* journal would also lead to economies and worthwhile simplifications. The political parties should consult with each other before nominating the Chairman of a new Committee of Inquiry, and the next Chairman of the BBC and IBA. Sir Hugh concluded his lecture with a forthright condemnation of the BBC Complaints Commission and the very idea of a broadcasting council. The governors should be 'restored to their proper role as trustees of the public interest'. While the majority of his suggestions might well have been accepted by the Conservative Government of the day, his last plea against a broadcasting council may well have come too late to gain acceptance, since the governors are seen by the public as defenders of their rival broadcasting organizations, and the governors' impartiality is suspect.

With the defeat of the Conservatives in the two 1974 general elections, the job of deciding what to do about broadcasting in the eighties fell to the Labour Party, who promptly reappointed the Committee of Inquiry under Lord Annan which they had first set up in 1970. At the time of publication, the results of the inquiry are not yet available, but their conclusions are likely to be reformist rather than radical. But one trend is clearly discernible in radical thinking; the demand for participation. This demand the Annan Committee of Inquiry will ignore at its peril.

Access and participation in broadcasting

No country recognizes a general right to broadcast. All wavelengths are licensed by the various national governments. Without government approval or the approval of those entrusted by government with the machinery of broadcasting control no one person or organization can demand the right to be heard (though the situation in Holland offers some fascinating opportunities).[20] However, in a democratic country like Britain, why should access to the media not be through the normal democratic processes? If freedom of political communication through the print media is like freedom of speech, a basic British liberty, why should there not be a similar freedom of access to television which has rapidly become a dominant means of political communication? Is it fair that certain groups of people with a political case of their own should be excluded from communicating through broadcasting?

Richard Crossman argued that politicians of all persuasions needed a forum of discussion that was not moulded by the preconceptions and practices of professionals in an entertainment medium.[21] He held that television treated even the major parties with superficial attention, typified by transmitting snippety quotations from speeches. Television news coverage trivialized the important political issues by sandwiching a five-minute interview on a defence White Paper or an important bill between two more 'entertaining' items. The exclusion today of non-official political groups such as the student radicals, and the republicans in Northern Ireland, results in acute problems for the country, as their contribution to the political debate is almost always denied until discontent boils over in violence onto the streets.

In 1972 Tony Benn put the case for breaking open the editorial unity of the broadcasting authorities. First, he wanted to enforce a direct right of access to the studios and ancillary facilities without the interference of 'professionals'. Any group with a message to deliver would have the right to deliver it, subject to the laws of libel and obscenity. Benn said, 'It is argued that the intervention of a professional communicator is necessary because ordinary people are so inarticulate and cannot be relied upon to express themselves clearly. But most people are very articulate when they are talking about what they know best.'[22] Later the success of the BBC *Open Door* programme proved that Benn was perfectly right in his assumptions. Still, *Open*

Door is more of a concession than a vital new development in broadcasting practice. Its late-night placing ensures that the audience is minimal.

Tony Benn had been one of the first to claim that coverage of union affairs by professional broadcasters was biassed and unfair. In January 1971 the ACTT published a survey of one week's television in which every single reference to the trades union movement on all three channels was examined for partiality on grounds of language, balance of views and balance of story elements. The conclusions were sombre indeed: 'Industrial affairs are covered in a superficial and haphazard fashion; [that] the BBC in particular scandalously failed to maintain impartiality in dealing with three issues during the week monitored; [that] ITV shows conscientious effort to achieve impartiality; [that] unions may be partly at fault in failing to supply news and check its coverage.'[23]

Later that year the TUC decided to set up a standing committee to study and report on the handling of trade union affairs on radio, television and the press. They planned to monitor broadcasts, to establish liaison with the press and to seek a process of public enquiry into the ownership and control of the mass media.[24] Tony Benn's second argument in favour of participation stated that if those concerned had no influence over the presentation of their case they could only be misrepresented.

Alerted to the need of some public statement to the Annan Committee, ACTT raised important points about the need for greater democracy in broadcasting. First, they demanded more access to information about the conduct of broadcasting for both the union and the public. Their report stated: 'The machinery of public trusteeship is invalidated if the trustees operate in secrecy and veil essential details of finance and policy decisions in the generalities of Annual Reports.' Next, they demanded the introduction of procedures of accountability: 'experiments could be started at once to extend the representation of the community in broadcasting organization'. Thirdly, they looked for a greater amount of internal democracy in broadcasting organization: 'we think the Union should seek a veto for workers over appointments and sackings in their departments'.[25]

Free communications depend on access, participation and democratic control – all so far only imperfectly conceptualized. British broadcasting has historically delegated such thorny problems to Royal Commissions. But Royal Commissions are limited both by their composition, and by their realization that too many radical recommendations will result in little being implemented by the government in power. Such was the fate of the Pilkington Commission's recommendations; such could be the fate that might befall the Annan Committee's proposals.

The Labour Party discussion document *The People and the Media* contained radical suggestions which make interesting reading. Most press attention was devoted to the sections that concerned newspapers and magazines, but the suggestions for the democratization of broadcasting were just as radical. The document began by stating that control of the media in a relatively few hands inevitably leads to a closed system of decision-making by unrepresentative groups. It was felt to be important 'to extend the degree to which those who work in the media can participate in decisions at every level, and have a chance to influence the general shape and tone of the publications or programmes with which they are connected'. The absence of external participation in programme-production under the present broadcasting systems led to bias against certain sections of the community. Most notable victims were the trade unions, as was proved by the ACTT research. The media generally, and broadcasting in particular, were failing to relate to society because they did not reflect a wide diversity of interests, preferring to confine themselves to the narrow middle ground of what the programme controllers considered safe and uncontroversial. What was needed were alternative structures for broadcasting, based on smaller units and more open decision-making. These would provide far more effective safeguards against government control than would any well-intentioned anonymous guardians.

Principles for extending democratic control in broadcasting

Any framework of control for broadcasting must provide safeguards against the twin enemies – government and commerce. The system should both be genuinely democratic and genuinely accountable. Fine as these ideals are, their implementation poses profound problems of restructuring the present institutions. *The People and the Media* proposed that all media should be placed on a public service basis, with all major broadcasting transmission equipment under public ownership. Funding would be centralized, depending on a combination of advertising and licence fee revenue. To give the widest possible access to the media to both individuals and community groups, decentralization of responsibility and controls would be encouraged. Perhaps most important of all for the future, all matters of government policy towards broadcasting and all decisions to be taken by the broadcasting authorities should be made public. Thus their implications could be considered by the public as a whole, and reactions fed back to the government and the broadcasting institutions through MPs, advisory bodies and public debate. The pamphlet reinforced Tony Benn's demands when it sought 'to develop the structures of democratic accountability within the mass media, and to allow greater influence to be exercised by those who work in them'. It also sought to 'improve the opportunity to publish and broadcast a diversity of views so as to eliminate any risk that the system might lead to government or commercial censorship'.[26]

The reactions of many broadcasters when reading these proposals was one of mild incredulity. How could such ideas possibly work in practice without a serious effect on the standards of broadcasting? Surely it was professionalism that had put British broadcasting where it was, at the head of the world league. To invite outside interference from non-professionals would be to invite disaster. What changes in broadcasting structure could possibly provide 'some permanent institutional expression of public involvement in the communications industries'?

The structural changes proposed were radical, but on the whole not so very different from the plans put forward by the advertisers themselves in the ISBA/IPA plans published in *Television 76*. Whereas the advertisers wanted a broadcasting council, the Labour Party wanted a communications council. Both had the function of drawing up rules for all sections of radio and television broadcasting. The communications council would look after film and the press as well – a daunting task. The communications council would have the second task of acting as an ombudsman in all complaints concerning television, radio or the press. In this capacity the council would have the right to demand air time or column space for the correction of errors of fact or redress of grievances. The council would have links with a National Consumers' Authority, and would include elected representatives from trade unions, local government and national organizations together with some MPs. The various eunuch-like BBC- and IBA-advisory bodies would be swept away. But in spite of its wide responsibilities, the communications council would still resemble these advisory bodies in one way – its role was advisory, not executive.

Whereas the ISBA/IPA plans assumed that the broadcasting council itself would control the four channels, two popular, one cultural and one educational, the Labour Party envisaged a completely new body, the Public Broadcasting Commission (PBC) to fund and control the four television channels. The PBC would not make programmes, but it would oversee general scheduling problems, and on occasion commission programmes or series of programmes of special public interest from independent organizations. The PBC would be fully independent of government, and, like the IBA at present, would decide guidelines on advertising, quotas of foreign material, and broadcasting hours. The PBC would fulfil the principles of democracy and accountability by containing elected representatives from major sections of the community. These would include elected representatives from the broadcasting organizations and local government, MPs, and nominees from important national organizations. PBC meetings would be public and all key decisions actively publicized.

With the communications council handling the development and the PBA the administration of national broadcasting policy, the actual programme-making would be carried out by a wide variety of dispersed units organized under two television corporations. Each corporation would have one national and one regional channel, using existing BBC and ITV facilities. There would also be two radio corporations, one taking over BBC Radio 1, 2, 3 and 4; the other taking over all local radio stations. Real internal democracy inside these small creative groups 'would enable broadcasting workers to contribute directly to the management and development of their own industry'.[27]

When it comes to finance, the two plans differ. Whereas the ISBA/IPA plans envisage the retention of licensing fees, the Labour Party want the PBC to determine how much should come direct from the Treasury and how much from advertising. Licensing would be phased out as being a clumsy and regressive tax. The claims that the licence fee ensures broadcasting's independence from government interference were felt to be unsubstantiated. Indeed, even given the principle underlying the licence fee, the government still has the power to decide when and by how much the fee should be raised – which can be a distinct limitation on the broadcasters' freedom of action.

Choices

The central problem remains for any committee entrusted with the duty of making recommendations for the future of British broadcasting: Should it, like all previous committees, decide to modify and adapt existing institutions, or should it recommend institutional change, and so run the risk that its recommendations will be largely ignored? Perhaps this time there is a real chance that the structures of broadcasting will be radically modified, and that when the Annan Committee reports, there will be a government in power with the necessary parliamentary majority and the determination to impose a new structure allowing both public access and participation. Perhaps in the event the stiffest opposition to change will come from the broadcasting organizations themselves. Even as clear-sighted a man as Sir Hugh Greene took years to come round to the view that real reforms are necessary.

Jeremy Isaacs of Thames Television, in an IBA public lecture in February 1975, argued that ITV companies had three distinct and very great advantages over the BBC; namely financial independence, diversity and small size. One can happily agree with him without believing, as he appears to do, that these admirable qualities can only exist within the present IBA system. They might exist still better in a system which was not unlike the Labour scheme outlined above, and where democratic dialogue about production policy could exist without the company sales staff attempting to intervene.

If the Annan Committee retain a federal structure for future British broadcasting, avoid the problems of outsize and over-centralized bureaucratic control, and yet preserve some of that BBC idealism about the purposes of broadcasting, they will have done well indeed. The members of the Annan Committee are not required to be brilliant innovators themselves. They have only to pay as much attention to the critics as to the defenders of the *status quo*, and to blend the best of the reformist measures with the best of the existing systems into a logical and cohesive plan. Many submissions have been made. It should not be beyond the wit of the Committee to come up with a sensible and workable package.

We may be disappointed when the Annan Committee has reported. If so, then will be the time for us to lobby the government of the day and demand that changes are made, new structures tried, and broadcasting given the new lease of life that it will so urgently need in 1981.

An Open Letter to Lord Annan

'You and your committee have been charged with a difficult task. Parliament has asked you to suggest how to set the guidelines for British broadcasting for the last quarter of the twentieth century. Multitudes of interested parties have deluged you with suggestions, recommendations and general advice. You are now charged with the task of finishing your report. I am afraid that few journalists and fewer government ministers will read the whole report, and that almost nobody outside the ranks of academics will read all the evidence. So the summary of your recommendations is by far the most important part of your work.

I shall be as brief as possible: you and other members of your committee are busy men and women and this Royal Commission is not your only commitment. You will see that I advocate the setting up of a permanent public Broadcasting Commission which will provide the recommendations for the next Royal Commission in the year AD 2000. I shall divide my recommendations into three groups of headings: structures, accountability and purpose.

Structures for broadcasting

1. *The position of the BBC.* The BBC should continue under a new charter to be responsible for two television channels and three radio wavelengths.

2. *The position of the IBA.* The IBA should continue to control independent radio and television companies. The IBA would be given powers to take over programming. No extra television channel would be awarded to the IBA, but IBA programme contractors would be able to sell pro-

grammes to the National Television Foundation (see below) if the NTF accepted them. One radio wavelength at present controlled by the BBC would be awarded to Independent Radio News for national coverage of news and current affairs with a built-in requirement for regional input from all independent radio stations. The IBA would be authorized to subsidize IRN if necessary.

3. *The National Television Foundation.* The fourth channel should be awarded to the National Television Foundation. This new form of public broadcasting authority should be a public body granted a charter by Parliament. This body would act primarily as a publisher for independent programme-makers of all kinds. It would be charged with the development of participatory structures to provide a greater measure of access to the screen, and participation in the control of programmes for the benefit of the public. Under its charter the NTF will be run by an elected or representative body of trustees, appointed with the permission of the Minister of Posts and Telecommunications. Its executive would be a small secretariat charged with creating a third force in British broadcasting. Programmes would be bought from independent programme-makers, from the IBA programme-contractors, from public bodies like the CBI and TUC, and from private-interest groups (of a non-commercial nature). The NTF would be financed by a proportion of the licence fee, at present paid *in toto* to the BBC, and by a percentage of the advertising levy on IBA programme-contractors. Its initial income should be £30 million per annum.

4. *Educational broadcasting.* Educational broadcasting should in future be financed and planned by the Department of Education and Science in conjunction with the Schools Broadcasting Council (which itself would then be financed by the DES). Programmes for schools would be produced by BBC and ITV producers as at present. The Open University would be similarly financed and would be broadcast on the fourth channel outside peak-hours.

5. *BBC/ITA competition*. Joint consultation between the BBC, IBA and NTF would ensure that direct competitive scheduling is avoided as a regular pattern. While it is perfectly permissible to have more than one channel covering events it is both wrong and wasteful to have *Panorama* on BBC 1 scheduled at the same time as *World in Action* on ITV, for example. BBC and ITV should alternate their coverage of major events like Wimbledon and the Olympics.

6. *Regional origination of programmes*. Both BBC and IBA companies must provide that a higher proportion of their programmes be originated from the regions. At present the BBC allows two network slots per week for regional contributions – there should be more. The advantages of decentralization for the BBC should be studied in the light of the BBC "Kensington House group" of producers' evidence already submitted to the Annan Committee (without the permission of BBC management). The IBA already has an excellent regional structure, but in practice the activities of the networking committee prevent it working as well as it should. IBA programming must ensure more networking of regional contributions. The NTF must also make sure that some of the programmes it buys are from independent film and television programme-makers in the regions.

7. *The licence fee system*. The licence fee system has helped preserve the independence of the BBC. The licence fee should be increased to provide BBC and NTF with adequate funds, and the fee should be index-linked, automatically rising annually to safeguard broadcasting from the effects of inflation.

8. *Appointment of governors of BBC, IBA, NTF*. In future the Crown should appoint the governors of BBC and IBA on the advice of a committee of the Privy Council, consisting of three members of the Cabinet, three members of the Opposition front bench, and four independent Privy

Councillors. The same committee will reserve a right to approve the nominations of the NTF Trustees. No BBC, IBA or NTF governor should be removed without the consent of the Commons.

9. *Political independence of BBC, IBA, NTF.* No government order to the broadcasting organizations should be issued without the consent of both Houses of Parliament, on a procedural motion that requires both notice and debate.

10. *Cable transmission and future technological developments.* The experimental cable services begun in five regions (Sheffield, Bristol, Greenwich, Swindon, Wellingborough) should be reactivated under IBA ownership, and other experiments, to a total of two dozen, be started if desired. To provide the necessary funds, the IBA should provide special funds, and bear ultimate responsibility for programme content, rather than the Home Office as formerly. The IBA should also be empowered to sell advertising on cable stations – rules would be those that apply to the ITV. Local authorities wanting to start their own cable station should be empowered to do so, subject to control by the IBA. No pay TV or subscription TV should be permitted for live programmes, but library access to videocassette programmes should be permitted on an experimental basis, under a general licence from the Public Broadcasting Commission.

11. *The Public Broadcasting Commission.* A new public body, the Public Broadcasting Commission, would be set up to conduct long-term research into broadcasting, to advise the government about future developments, and to provide a centre to ensure accountability within broadcasting. The Public Broadcasting Commission (PBC) would be controlled by a Council, elected by the interests which it represented, and under the ultimate jurisdiction of trustees appointed by the Committee of the Privy Council which appoints the governors of BBC and IBA. The

PBC would have a suitably qualified secretariat, made up of a permanent director, six second-tier staff from the fields of interest covered by the specialist panels on aspects of broadcasting, a research and survey team of four members, executive and clerical staff. The PBC would provide a central Programme Complaints Tribunal, a Technical Standards Committee, and would own and run all transmission equipment at transmitters at present owned and run by the IBA and BBC. It would be funded by fees charged for the use of transmitters. The estimated cost of running the centre is put at one million pounds a year; surplus revenues would go to the NTF.

Accountability

12. *The Public Broadcasting Commission: functions.* The primary method for ensuring accountability to the public by broadcasters would be through the Public Broadcasting Commission. The PBC, financed by revenue from transmission-equipment ownership, would be responsible for the three "R's" of television – Research, Reviews and Rebukes. The necessity of long-term in-depth research into television is widely admitted; the PBC would initiate a wide range of such projects. As a central review body, the PBC would occupy the middle ground between government and the broadcasting institutions. It should keep under constant review the art, philosophy, content and practice of broadcasting, having particular regard to its social effects. It would promote public understanding and debate any issue concerned with the broadcasting services. It would undertake, promote or co-ordinate, at the request of government, the broadcasting organizations or other clients, research into particular aspects of broadcasting.

13. *The Public Broadcasting Commission: accountability.* The PBC would be as democratic a body as possible. Members would be nominated or elected by local and regional authorities, national social welfare and cultural organizations, educational bodies, the churches, the trade unions, industry, humanist organizations, government, broadcast-

ing institutions, and representatives from nine regional committees of not more than six members. Each would provide a professional commentary on those matters affecting broadcasting which touch on community and social affairs, the arts and sciences, the technical sphere of transmission, formal and adult education, and entertainment.

14. *The Public Broadcasting Commission: the programme complaints board.* Complaints by the general public generally fall into three categories. The first group of complainants are those who protest because they consider that too many programmes offend accepted standards of morals and manners. The second category of complainants are those who complain about misrepresentation of facts and opinions, and the unfair treatment of those who appear on radio and television. The third category are those who fear that the social effects of television may be harmful to the future development of society. They complain of programming excessively weighted in favour of entertainment, the promotion of false values and the glamourization of violence, acquisitiveness, the trivial and the superficial.

The Programme Complaints Commission would be concerned with the second category of complainant and take over the BBC and IBA complaint structures. The PCC would have the sole duty to consider charges of inaccuracy and misrepresentation made against the BBC, the IBA and the NTF, but only if those institutions failed to satisfy the complainant, and without prejudice to the complainant's rights in law. Adjudications would be published, and the broadcasters would be required to make an on-air apology if found guilty of misrepresentation.

Questions of taste, and complaints about morals and manners would however not be a subject for the PCC. Standards of taste cannot be a subject of legislation, and the broadcasting organizations should be left to censor their own programmes. Complainants should address complaints about taste to the governors of the organizations concerned. Those who complain about the social effects of television would be carefully heeded by those responsible for research into the long-term effects of television. The standing committee into the social effects of television would be required to make an annual report to the PBC.

15. *Accountability of individuals.* There is some evidence that a well-known commentator has accepted secret retainer fees. It is desirable that all commentators declare their interests in a document published annually, that lists these in the same form as the MPs' register of interests. Producers of financial programmes would not be allowed to handle their own share portfolios – such control should be handed over to a merchant bank to act on their behalf.

Purpose in broadcasting

16. *Entertainment, information and education.* The aims of broadcasting have been traditionally enshrined in the three aspects of broadcasting – entertainment, information and education. This has proved a practical and flexible statement of aims, within which broadcasters have found room for adaptation and change.

Of the three, entertainment is the most popular, and provides the biggest audience, so sought after by advertisers and programme-controllers. The danger is that entertainment is allotted too much air-time, or, worse, that serious matters are trivialized by the relentless application of 'showbiz' values. On all three channels at present facts are too often distorted for the sake of colourful treatment, serious issues are entrusted to lively but ill-informed speakers, complex questions are over-simplified and questions which have puzzled mankind for centuries are rationed to a few moments' discussion. The results of such practices can be educationally bad, a distortion of the truth, and only marginally entertaining.

17. *Broadcasting as an instrument of social change.* It is pertinent to point out that broadcasters have been too exclusively concerned with the effects on and benefits to the individual viewer or listener, and only indirectly with its effects on society as a whole. But contemporary thinkers are

increasingly aware that broadcasting is, accidentally or by design, an instrument of social change. They question to what social purposes it should be directed for the common good, and what effects it may unintentionally produce if not so directed. This raises the question of ultimate purpose, not only for broadcasting, but for society. However, many of those who work in broadcasting, and, more importantly, those who control it, would deny that social purpose is any concern of theirs, or that broadcasting does indeed affect national purpose. This is a cause for some concern.

18. *Broadcasting and the needs of society.* Increasingly broadcasting has failed to rise to the challenges of our changing society. It no longer reflects a wide diversity of interests, preferring to confine itself to the safe middle-ground of what programme-controllers consider generally acceptable and uncontroversial. We may be told that we live in a free society, but in fact we live in an increasingly closed system, in which the secrecy which surrounds government is reflected by the broadcasting organizations. Control of broadcasting in so few hands has led to a closed system of decision-making, by small cliques representing no one but themselves. These problems of exclusivity and secrecy can only be solved by developing the structures of democratic accountability within broadcasting, and by allowing greater influence to be exercised by those who work as broadcasters.

19. *Broadcasting and a more participatory national democracy.* Those who run television cannot and should not take political and social decisions on behalf of the people. But they can greatly assist people to make the best possible contribution to the decisions made on their behalf by their elected representatives. Television can be a forum of debate on the goals of society, and can analyse the existing social institutions. It can explore gaps and breakdowns in society and society's existing social institutions. It can reveal what needs to be done and how results might be

achieved. In a special way, it can give a voice to the voiceless, can spotlight the obscure and the downtrodden.

19. *The importance of genuine information.* Communications are the life-blood of a community as complex as ours. The individual rightly believes that he has less and less control over the remote, all-powerful political and commercial institutions, the ramifications of bureaucracy and the advances of technology. Television has an absolute social duty to give more factual information more intelligibly about the large national issues – like Concorde – and the smaller local issues – like redevelopment. For too long sensationalism has been an all-powerful news value, at the expense of significance. Bitty, breathless and disconnected presentation of news and current affairs must make way for more analytical forms, for further and better-researched investigatory journalism, for a rigorous avoidance of news-stereotyping of current issues, especially in the field of industrial relations.

20. *Aims and ideals.* Allowing for divergences of belief and behaviour in our multi-credal society, there is still a consensus about what is human and what is inhuman. You do not have to be a Socialist to believe that cruelty, greed, selfishness, poverty and oppression are wrong. You do not have to be a Christian to believe that compassion, generosity, honesty, tolerance and consideration for others are highly desirable human qualities. Broadcasters, while they have a duty to explore the dark and dangerous manifestations of man, also have a duty to illuminate and foster the highest human ideals, and many individual programmes already do this.

But the cumulative pattern of broadcasting implants the opposite ideals. Patterns of programming involving massive distortion of human values are not helpful for the growth of the just society. We are given programmes where heroes and villains alike only triumph by being better at violence; where commercial materialism and the life of the very rich is held out to be the right goal for all citizens;

where "personalities" and their views are held to be more important than people and their opinions. The broadcasters here fail not only themselves; they fail the society that appointed them. Since the potential educative effect of broadcasting is so great, it must be at least as concerned about the moral, social and political influences of programming as schools are about the moral, social and political influences of the education they offer.

I conclude with the words of a great broadcaster, Edward R. Murrow: "This instrument can teach, it can illuminate; yes, and it can even inspire. But it can only do so to the extent that humans are determined to use it to those ends. Otherwise it is merely lights and wires in a box." '

Notes

Chapter One

1 *BBC Audience Research*, 1974/75.
2 James McMillan, *The Roots of Corruption*, Tom Stacey, 1972.
3 Gavin Reid, *The Elaborate Funeral*, Hodder and Stoughton, 1972.
4 Brian Groombridge, *Television and the People – A Programme for Democratic Participation*, Penguin, 1972.
5 ACTT Television Commission, *One Week – A survey of Television Coverage of Union and Industrial Affairs*, January 1971.
6 Herbert Marcuse, *One-Dimensional Man*, Routledge and Kegan Paul, 1964; paperback, Sphere Books, 1968.
7 Stuart Hood, 'The Politics of Television' in *Sociology of Mass Communications*, edited by Dennis McQuail, Penguin, 1972.
8 *The Open Secret*, 1968.

Chapter Two

1 Peter Black, *The Mirror in the Corner*, Hutchinson, 1972.
2 Peter Black, *The Biggest Aspidistra in the World*, BBC, 1972.
3 Lord Reith, *Broadcast Over Britain*, Hodder and Stoughton, 1974.

Chapter Three

1 H. H. Wilson, *Pressure Group – The Campaign for Commercial Television*, Secker and Warburg, 1961.
2 Richard Rose, 'The Influence of the Media' in *Studies in British Politics*, MacMillan, 1966.

Chapter Four

1 *Report of the Committee on Broadcasting*, 1960 (The 'Pilkington Report'), HMSO, June 1962.
2 Peter Black, *The Mirror in the Corner*, Hutchinson, 1972.
3 *The Mirror in the Corner*.
4 Sir Hugh Greene, *The Third Floor Front*, Bodley Head, 1969.
5 *The Third Floor Front*.

Chapter Five

1 The suggestive title of a book by Joan Bakewell and Nicholas Garnham.
2 Anthony Smith, *The Shadow in the Cave*, Allen and Unwin, 1974.
3 *Principles and Practices in Documentary Programmes*, BBC, April 1972.
4 *The Third Floor Front*.
5 Robin Day, *Day by Day*, William Kimber, 1975.
6 T. H. White, *The Making of the President, 1968*, Jonathan Cape, 1969.

Chapter Six

1 Robert MacNeil, *The People Machine*, Eyre and Spottiswoode, 1970.
2 Kurt and Gladys Engel Lang, *Politicians and Television*, Quadrangle Books, Chicago, 1968.
3 *The People Machine*.
4 Milton Shulman, *The Ravenous Eye*, Cassell, 1973.
5 Arthur Schlesinger in *American Television Guide*, 22 October 1966.
6 *The Ravenous Eye*.
7 *Newsweek*, 20 November 1972.
8 *Time*, 8 July 1974.
9 *Politicians and Television*.

10 J. Trenaman and D. McQuail, *Television and the Political Image*, Methuen, 1961.
11 David Dimbleby, 'A Broadcaster's Hopes', *The Listener*, 16 November 1972.
12 John Dearlove, 'The BBC and the Politicians', *Index* No. 1, 1974.
13 Martin Harrison, 'Broadcasting' in Butler and Pinto-Duschinsky, *The British General Election of 1970*, MacMillan, 1971.
14 Anthony Smith, 'Broadcasting', in David Butler and Uwe Kitzinger, *The Referendum 1975*, MacMillan, 1976.
15 Trevor Pateman, 'Television and the February 1974 General Election', BFI Television Monograph, British Film Institute.

Chapter Seven

1 *Broadcasting, Society and the Church*, Church Information Office, 1973.
2 *The Third Floor Front*.
3 *The Listener*, 3 October 1968
4 *The Listener*, 3 October 1968.

Chapter Eight

1 C. Wright Mills, *The Power Elite*, OUP New York, 1956.
2 M. McLuhan, *Understanding Media*, Routledge and Kegan Paul, 1964; paperback Sphere Books 1967.
3 Alan Hancock, *Mass Communication*, Longmans, 1968.
4 Raymond Williams, *Television – Technology and Cultural Form*, Fontana, 1974.
5 Mrs Grace Wyndham Goldie, in *Society of Film and Television Arts Journal*, October 1974.
6 *PEP Report on Television*, 1965.
7 Roderick Kedward, *The Oxford History of the Twentieth Century*, Notes to accompany pilot video-tapes, OUP, 1971.
8 Elmo Roper and Associates, *New trends in the public's*

measure of Television and Other Media, Television
Information Office, New York, 1965.
9 Independent Television Authority, London, 1966.

Chapter Nine

1 Robert Heron, *Society of Film and Television Arts*,
Journal No. 45, Autumn 1971.
2 Brenda Maddox, *Beyond Babel*, Andre Deutsch, 1972.
3 Congressman James Fulton of Pennsylvania at
Congressional Hearings on the subject of Satellite
Broadcasting, 1969.
4 Edgaro Galli, *ITC Telecommunication Journal*, May
1970.

Chapter Ten

1 Malcolm Muggeridge in *Pornography – The Longford
Report*, Hodder and Stoughton, 1972.
2 Mary Whitehouse, *Who Does She Think She Is?*, New
English Library, 1971.
3 *Who Does She Think She Is?*
4 Lord Hill, *Behind the Screen*, Sidgwick and Jackson, 1974.
5 *Who Does She Think She Is?*
6 Anthony Smith, *British Broadcasting*, David and Charles,
1974.
7 *Memorandum on the Report of the Broadcasting
Committee, 1949* (Beveridge Report), Cmd. 8291, 1950–51
XXVII, 19, paras 14–17.
8 Barbara Wootton, *In a World I Never Made*, Allen and
Unwin, 1967.
9 Lord Normanbrook, *The Functions of the BBC's
Governors*, BBC Lunchtime Lectures, 4th Series No. 3,
10–12.
10 Sir Hugh Greene, *The Third Floor Front*, Bodley Head,
1969.
11 Lord Hill's speech to the Rotary Club of London, 13 May
1964 (*ITA Notes* No. 5, June 1964).

12 *Behind the Screen.*
13 *Broadcasting and the Public Mood* (BBC Internal Paper, 1968).
14 *Behind the Screen.*
15 *Behind the Screen.*
16 *Behind the Screen.*
17 *Report of the Broadcasting Committee 1949* (Beveridge Report), p. 166 para 552, Cmd. 8116, HMSO.
18 *The Functions of the BBC's Governors.*
19 *Behind the Screen.*
20 *The Portrayal of Violence in Television Programmes*, BBC, March 1972. *Principle and Practice in News and Current Affairs* and *Principles and Practice in Documentary Programmes*, BBC.
21 Julian Critchley, *Council for Broadcasting*, Conservative Political Centre, 1971.
22 *The Times*, Law Report, 5 February 1973.
23 *The Report of the Broadcasting Committee* (Beveridge Report), 1949. Reprint, Appendix E, p. 282.

Chapter Eleven

1 *Report of the Committee on Broadcasting 1960* (Pilkington Committee), HMSO, June 1962.
2 *Pilkington Report.*
3 J. D. Halloran, R. L. Brown, D. C. Chaney, *Television and Delinquency*, Leicester University Press, 1970.
4 Milton Shulman, *The Ravenous Eye*, Cassell, 1973.
5 Television Research Committee on Television and Delinquency *Second Progress Report and Recommendations*, Leicester University Press, 1969.
6 H. T. Himmelweit, A. N. Oppenheim, P. Vince, *Television and the Child*, OUP, 1958.
7 Personal interview with Richard Salent in January 1969, quoted in Milton Shulman, *The Ravenous Eye*.
8 BBC Audience Research *Report on Violence in Television* March 1972.
9 David Attenborough, *The Portrayal of Violence in Television Programmes* – A Note of Guidance, pages 12–13, March 1972.

10 *Violence in Television Programmes* – The ITV Code, ITA, October 1971.
11 Lord Hill, *Behind the Screen*.
12 *BBC Handbook*, 1969.
13 Julian Critchley, *Council for Broadcasting*, Conservative Political Centre, January 1971.
14 *Television 76*, Incorporated Society of British Advertisers and Institute of Practitioners in Advertising, November 1972.
15 *Television 76*.
16 *ITV 2: Submission to the Minister of Posts and Telecommunications*, ITA, December 1971.
17 *Second Report from the Select Committee on Nationalized Industries*, Session 1971–2, House of Commons Paper 465, September 1972, lxix–lxxii, para. 171.
18 George Wedell, *Broadcasting and Public Policy*, Michael Joseph, 1968.
19 Sir Hugh Greene, Granada *Guildhall Lecture*, reprinted in *New Statesman*, 20 October 1972.
20 Timothy Green, *The Universal Eye – World Television in the Seventies*, Bodley Head, 1972.
21 Richard Crossman, *The Politics of Television: TV and the Political Party Image* (published version of the Granada *Guildhall Lecture*, 1969).
22 *The Fourth Symposium on Broadcasting Policy*, University of Manchester, 1972.
23 *ACTT Television Commission, One Week – A Survey of Television Coverage of Union and Industrial Affairs*, January 1971.
24 Resolution No. 16 of Trades Union Congress, 1971.
25 *ACTT Television Commission Report* to Annual Conference, 1972.
26 *The People and the Media*.
27 *Broadcast*, February 1975.

Index